AF600043

A COMPARATIVE STUDY OF THE CONSTITUTION "APOSTOLICAE SEDIS" AND THE "CODEX JURIS CANONICI"

A DISSERTATION

SUBMITTED TO

THE FACULTY OF SACRED SCIENCES OF THE CATHOLIC UNIVERSITY OF AMERICA

IN PARTIAL FULFILMENT OF THE REQUIREMENTS FOR THE DEGREE OF

DOCTOR OF CANON LAW

BY

THE REV. GEORGE LEO LEECH, J. C. L.

OF THE ARCHDIOCESE OF PHILADELPHIA

1922

NIHIL OBSTAT:
+THOMAS JOSEPH SHAHAN, S. T. D.
Censor Deputatus.

IMPRIMATUR:
+M. J. CURLEY, D. D.,
Archiepiscopus Baltimorensis.

UNIVERSITAS CATHOLICA AMERICAE
WASHINGTONII

SACRA FACULTAS THEOLOGICA
1921-1922
No. 15

CONTENTS

SOURCES

(The decrees cited in the dissertation will be found among the following works.)

CORPUS JURIS CANONICI. (Richter) Lipsiae, 1839.

CANONES ET DECRETA CONCILII TRIDENTINI. Romae, 1904.

BENED. P. XIV, BULLARIUM. Mechliniae, 1826.

BULLARIUM ROMANUM. Aug.-Taurin, 1846-1872.

BULLARII ROMANI CONTINUATIO. Prati, 1846-1856.

PII IX P.M. ACTA. Romae, 1846-1878.

ACTA SANCTAE SEDIS. Romae, 1865-1908.

ACTA APOSTOLICAE SEDIS. Romae, 1909-1921.

COLLECTANEA S. CONG. DE PROP. FIDE (1622-1906). Romae, 1907.

ACTA ET DECRETA CONC. PLEN. BALT. II. Baltimorae, 1868.

ACTA ET DECRETA CONC. PLEN. BALT. III. Baltimorae, 1886.

CODEX JURIS CANONICI. Romae, 1917.

BIBLIOGRAPHY

(The works listed below will, after being mentioned for the first time, be cited by the name of the author only. If several works of the same author are used the title of the particular work will be mentioned in each case.)

AMERICAN ECCLESIASTICAL REVIEW (Vol. LVI-LXVI). Philadelphia.

IRISH ECCLESIASTICAL RECORD (Fifth series, Vol. IX-XVIII). Dublin.

IRISH THEOLOGICAL QUARTERLY (Vol. XII-XXI). Dublin.

AERTNYS, *Theologia Moralis.* Tornaci, 1893.

AICHNER, *Compendium Juris Ecclesiastici.* Brixinae, 1887.

ALPHONSUS S., *Theologia Moralis.* Ratisbonae, 1846.

ANTONELLI, *Medicina Pastoralis.* Romae, 1920.

AUGUSTINE, *A Commentary on the New Code of Canon Law.* St. Louis, 1918.

AVANZINI, *De Const. "Apost. Sedis."* Romae, 1872.

AYRINHAC, *Penal Legislation in the New Code of Canon Law.* New York, 1920.

BALLERINI-PALMIERI, *Tractatus de Censuris.* Prati, 1893.

BARGILLIAT, *Praelectiones Juris Canonici.* Parisiis, 1913.

BLAT, *Commentarium Textus Codicis Juris Canonici.* Romae, 1919.

BUCCERONI, *Commentarium in Const. "Apost. Sedis."* Romae, 1892.

CAPELLO, *De Censuris.* Aug. Taurin, 1919.
De Curia Romana. Romae, 1911.

CARR, *The Const. "Apost. Sedis Moderationi."* Dublin, 1879.

CATHOLIC ENCYCLOPEDIA (quoted by title of article). New York, 1907.

CAVIGLIOLI, *Censurae Latae Sententiae.* Romae, 1920.

CERATO, *Censurae Vigentes.* Patavia, 1918.

CHELODI, *Jus Matrimoniale,* Ed. 3a. Tridenti, 1921.
Jus Poenale. Tridenti, 1920.

COCCHI, *Commentarium in Codicem Juris Canonici.* Aug.-Taur., 1922.

D'ANNIBALE, *Summa Theologiae Moralis.* Romae, 1891.
Commentarium in Const. "Apost. Sedis." Prati, 1894.

DE SMET, *De Sponsalibus et Matrimonio.* Brugis, 1920.

EICHMAN, *Das Strafgesetz des "Codex Juris Canonici."* Paderborn, 1920.

ESCHBACH, *Disputationes Physiologico-Theologicae*, Ed. 3a. Romae.

FERRERES, *Institutiones Canonicae.* Barcinonae, 1917.

Compendium Theologiae Moralis. Barcinonae, 1918.

GASPARRI, *Tractatus Canonicus de Matrimonio.* Parisiis, 1904.

Tractatus Canonicus de Sacra Ordinatione. Parisiis, 1893.

GENICOT, *Institutiones Theologiae Moralis.* Bruxellis, 1921.

HINSCHIUS, *System des Katholischen Kirchenrechts.* Berlin, 1888.

HOLLWECK, *Die Kirchlichen Strafgesetze.* Mainz, 1899.

LEGA, *Praelectiones in Textum Juris Canonici.* Romae, 1910.

LEHMKUHL, *Theologia Moralis*, Ed. 4a. Friburgi Brisgoviae, 1887.

NOLDIN-SCHONEGGER, *De Poenis Ecclesiasticis.* Oeniponte, 1821.

OJETTI, *De Romana Curia.* Romae, 1910.

Synopsis Rerum Moralium et Juris Pontificii. Romae, 1914.

PASTOR, *History of the Popes.* St. Louis, 1899.

PAPI, *The Government of Religious Communities.* New York, 1919.

PENNACCHI, *Commentarium in Const. "Apost. Sedis."* Romae, 1883.

REIFFENSTUEL, *Jus Canonicum Universum.* Venetiis, 1726.

SABETTI-BARRETT, *Compendium Theologiae Moralis*, Ed. 26a. New York, 1917.

SCHMALZGRUEBER, *Jus Ecclesiasticum Universum.* Romae, 1845.

SEBASTIANELLI, *Praelectiones Juris Canonici.* Romae, 1905.

SEBASTIANI, *Summarium Theologiae Moralis,* Ed. 5a. Romae, 1920.

SLATER, *A Manual of Moral Theology.* New York, 1908.

SMITH, *Elements of Ecclesiastical Law.* New York, 1877.

SOLE, *De Delictis et Poenis.* Romae, 1920.

SUAREZ, *De Censuris.* Parisiis, 1866.

TAUNTON, *Law of the Church.* London, 1906.

TEPHANY, *Constitution "Apost. Sedis."* Tours, 1883.

VECCHIOTTI, *Institutiones Canonicae.* Aug.-Taurin, 1886.

VLAMING, *Praelectiones Juris Matrimonii.* Bussum in Hollandia, 1919.

WERNZ, *Jus Decretalium.* Prati, 1915.

INTRODUCTION

Coactive power is an essential attribute of sovereignty. In vain does a government enact laws and administer justice if it is unable to carry its laws and mandates into execution. All three powers are necessary for the due conservation of public order and the efficacious attainment of the end of society. The Church, then, being a perfect society, rightfully claims and enjoys, independently of any human authority, the right to exact obedience from her members, even by compulsion.

This right is indispensable to the Church. For, although of divine origin, the Church is made up of human members, weak, erring and beset with human passions. Whence arises the need of disciplinary laws for their guidance and of penalties for their correction. Now, from the very nature of these laws it will be seen that they cannot well remain constant. The dogmatic teaching of the Church is, indeed, infallible and, when once proposed, immutable. Her strictly disciplinary laws, however, must vary with the varying requirements of different ages. On the one hand, the Church has to legislate for every time and for every place; on the other, she finds perpetual change going on within her wide domain. The wants, the weaknesses, the errors, the crimes of one century or generation differ widely from those of another; yet the Church's maternal duty towards her children remains the same, and for these wants, weaknesses, errors and crimes her legislation must at all times be suitable.[1]

Wherefore the Church has consistently vindicated her right to alter her disciplinary laws according as the welfare of her children or the spirit of the times seemed to require. A noteworthy instance is found in the Decrees of the Council of Trent, Sess. XXI, cap. 2, de ref.[2].

1 Cf. Cavagnis, "Institutiones Juris Publ. Ecclesiasticae," Romae, 1906, I. n. 60 ss.

2 "Praeterea declarat—Sancta Synodus—hanc potestatem perpetuo in Ecclesia fuisse, ut in Sacramentorum dispensatione, salva illorum substantia, ea statueret, vel mutaret, quae suscipientium utilitati, seu ipsorum Sacramentorum venerationi, pro rerum, temporum et locorum varietate, magis expedire judicaret."

When, in the course of ages, laws become multiplied and consequently complicated, while the circumstances that called them forth have ceased to exist or have become considerably modified, prudence suggests to wise rulers, in both Church and State, the expediency of revising or of abolishing them, so as to remove unnecessary restraints, secure uniformity of practice and ensure the tranquility of consciences.

Of the numerous disciplinary reforms instituted during the singularly long and eventful pontificate of Pope Pius IX, one of the most useful and practical was the limitation and classification of Censures which was effected by the Constitution *Apostolicae Sedis*, promulgated October 12, 1869. In the course of centuries, whose every year presented fresh legislative needs, the penal statutes of the Church had accumulated to enormous proportions, some confirming, some modifying, some abrogating laws that had previously been established. This discipline was, it is true, simplified considerably by the Council of Trent. (1545-1563.) Indeed, the greater part of the Tridentine legislation finds confirmation in the *Codex Juris Canonici*. But, as in the centuries preceding the great Council, so too in those which followed it, the needs of new laws, of alterations and of abrogations continued to arise and were duly satisfied. Thus again the Church found her penal statutes numerous and complicated—a source of confusion to canonists, of perplexity to moralists and, only too frequently, a cause of scrupulosity among the faithful.[3]

Now, it is chiefly in regard to punishments that are set down in the common law and are incurred *ipso facto* that anxieties may arise, and particularly in regard to censures—excommunication, suspension and interdict—whereby the children of the Church, cleric and lay, are deprived, in greater or lesser degree, of the spiritual means which they normally should enjoy. Accordingly, it was to censures incurred *ipso facto ipsoque jure* that

3 Const. *Apost. Sedis.*

Pius IX directed his attention when he determined that the legislation of three hundred years' growth must be simplified. By the Const. *Apost. Sedis* he recast the list of such censures, declaring, directly or indirectly, which of these were to obtain thenceforth, all others being abrogated by their very omission. The need which this Constitution was intended to supply is sufficiently indicated in the following words of the Constitution itself:

> ". . . Cum animo Nostro jampridem revolveremus, ecclesiasticas censuras, quae per modum latae sententiae, ipsoque facto incurrendae ad incolumitatem ac disciplinam ipsius Ecclesiae tutandam, effraenamque improborum licentiam coercendam et emendandam sancte per singulas aetates indictae ac promulgatae sunt, magnum ad numerum sensim excrevisse; quasdam etiam, temporibus moribusque mutatis, a fine atque causis, ob quas impositae fuerant, vel a pristina utilitate, atque opportunitate excidisse; eamque ob rem non infrequentes oriri sive in iis, quibus animarum cura commissa est, sive in ipsis fidelibus dubietates, anxietates, angoresque conscientiae; Nos ejusmodi incommodis occurrere volentes, plenam earundem recensionem fieri, Nobisque proponi jussimus, ut diligenti adhibita consideratione, statueremus, quasnam ex illis servare ac retinere oporteret, quas vero moderari, abrogare congrueret. . ."

It is seen from the foregoing that in the Const. *Apost. Sedis* there was question only of censures, i. e., those punishments whose primary end is the emendation, rather than the punishment, of the delinquent.[4] Moreover, not all of these are dealt with in that Constitution, but only

4 It is curious to observe that, although a censure is essentially medicinal and ought, in justice, to be terminated when the delinquent has manifested amendment by receding from his contumacy, yet several of the suspensions enumerated in the Constitution of Pius IX (in whose time the nature of censure was quite clearly defined) were made to continue for a definite time or *ad beneplacitum*. These were therefore, *vindictive* rather than medicinal punishments. Cf. cann. 2242, 2286. Perhaps this accounts for Hollweck's contention that the medicinal quality is not essential to a censure. See "Die Kirchlichen Strafgesetze," Mainz, 1899, par. 22. Such an opinion, singular as it was in recent times, is absolutely incompatible with the Code. Cf. Hinschius, "System des Katholischen Kirchenrechts," Berlin, 1888, IV, 748, ss.

the censures which are so attached to the violation of a law that (a) the delinquent incurs the censures in the very act of breaking the law and (b) the censure binds his conscience at once without the process of a trial or the formality of a judicial sentence. For it is in such cases—where no time intervenes between the act of delinquency and the imposition of the penalty—that the minds of the faithful might find occasion for anxieties and perplexities. The Constitution, then, did not alter the so-called censures *ferendae sententiae,* which bind the subject only when the ecclesiastical judge has duly pronounced the condemnatory sentence; nor did it affect censures *ab homine,* which are imposed by way of particular precept or condemnatory sentence, even though the censures be already stipulated in the letter of the law.

Finally, there were three classes of censures already existing which, although they were not recited specifically in the Constitution, were declared by Pius IX[5] to retain their force even after the promulgation of the Constitution. These were (a) the censures incurred for crimes committed in connection with the election of the Roman Pontiff; (b) the censures regarding the internal government of Orders and Institutes of Regulars, Colleges, Congregations, and other Pious Associations and Places; and (c) the censures directly instituted by the Fathers of the Council of Trent.[6] Indeed, these censures were declared to have the same force as if they were for the first time established and promulgated by the Constitution *Apost. Sedis.*[7]

There were, therefore, after the promulgation of the Const. *Apost. Sedis,* four classes or groups of censures, to be incurred *ipso jure ipsoque facto,* which enjoyed the force of the common law: 1. those specifically recited in

5 Const. cit.

6 With one exception, q. v. in Chap. IV, Art. V.

7 ". . . simul declarantes, easdem non modo ex veterum canonum auctoritate, quatenus cum hac Nostra Constitutione conveniunt, verum etiam ex hac ipsa Constitutione Nostra, non secus ac si primum editae ab ea fuerint, vim suam prorsus accipere debere."

the Constitution itself (46 in number); 2. those directly enacted by the Council of Trent (19); 3. those regarding the election of the Roman Pontiff (7); 4. those imposed for the internal government of Orders and Institutes of Regulars, etc. (4).

The year 1917 will ever stand out prominently in the history of Canonical legislation. For it saw the fulfillment of a desire of centuries when His Holiness Benedict XV, of happy memory, on Pentecost of that year gave to the Church the *Codex Juris Canonici*, in which the disciplinary laws of the Latin Church, the obsolete and the useless having been abrogated and new ones meeting the conditions of our time inserted, are digested in remarkably lucid and concise order and presented to the faithful in one volume.[8] In this recent codification the censure law, with which Pius IX dealt so thoroughly, is, of course, again concerned. A number of the censures which that Pontiff saw fit to insert in his exclusive list have, even in this comparatively brief lapse of time, been deemed obsolete or inopportune, and are, by their omission from the new Code, abrogated.[9] Others have been modified, being made less or more severe, restricted or extended, according as conditions of the present day and provision for future needs have seemed to require.

As regards censures *latae sententiae*, the Const. *Apost. Sedis* was the law of the Church for the fifty years prior to the new Code. If, therefore, any changes in that law have been effected by the Code—and indeed there have been—it is important that they be ascertained. It is principally to the exposition of these changes that we bend our efforts in the present work, instituting a comparison between the Const. *Apost. Sedis* and the *Codex Juris Canonici* in order thereby to show to what extent the law of 1869 is confirmed or modified or abrogated.

A word should be added regarding the form adopted for the present dissertation. The "S. Congr. de Seminariis et de Studiorum Universitatibus" by its decree

8 Codex I. C. p. xxxi.
9 Can. 6, n. 5.

"Cum Novum," dated Aug. 7, 1917, prescribed that thenceforth in treatises on Canon Law the order of the Code, by title and chapter, should be followed. Now, in the Const. *Apost. Sedis* the censures were divided into groups of *excommunications, suspensions* and *interdicts* and were classified according to the manner in which they were reserved, viz. *speciali modo, simpliciter*, etc. In the new Code, however, a different norm has been followed. Here the censures, as also the lesser penalties, which are inflicted for specific delinquencies are classified according to the *nature* of the respective delinquencies. Since, therefore, the present work is one of comparison, by which we endeavor to ascertain the changes which the new law has made in what previously obtained, it has been deemed more expedient to follow herein the order of the Constitution of Pius IX, whose articles we shall cite by series and number, bringing into juxtaposition with each article the canon or canons of the Code, if such there be, which now constitute the law in the given case.

In their respective places will be likewise treated the censures imposed by the Council of Trent and confirmed by the Constitution, those relating to the election of the Roman Pontiff and those to the internal government of Orders and Institutes of Regulars, etc. Nine censures enacted subsequent to the Const. *Apost. Sedis* and prior to the Code will also be treated. Finally, in order that we may afford a conspectus of the censures *latae sententiae* that are now in force by the common law, we shall subjoin, in their proper places, respectively, any censures which have been newly established by the Code itself.

CHAPTER I

Excommunications Reserved "Speciali Modo" to the Apostolic See

The censures of excommunication contained in the Const. *Apost. Sedis* are divided into four classes, the norm of division being, as we have already stated, the manner in which these were reserved. Accordingly, the four classes are: 1. those reserved to the Roman Pontiff *speciali modo;* 2. those reserved to him *simpliciter;* 3. those reserved to the Ordinary; and 4. those not reserved. In the present chapter the excommunications of the first class will be dealt with. Of these there are twelve, all of which, except the tenth, were contained in the well-known Bull, *In Coena Domini* or the *Bulla Coenae.*[1] To these we shall subjoin the two censures likewise reserved, which came into existence after the publication of the Const. of 1869[2] and four which are found for the first time in the new Code, two of which are reserved *specialissimo modo* to the Holy See.

Art. I. Const. *Apostolicae Sedis:*

> **"Itaque excommunicationi latae sententiae speciali modo Romano Pontifici reservatae subjacere declaramus:**
>
> **"Omnes a christiana fide apostatas, et omnes et singulos haereticos, quocunque nomine censeantur, et cujuscunque sectae existant, eisque credentes,**

1 So named from the fact that it was read publicly in Rome each year on Holy Thursday, up to the year 1770, when it was discontinued. It is not known by whom it was originally drawn up, but it was certainly in existence and published annually in the early part of the fifteenth century. It was formally abrogated by the Const. *Apost. Sedis.* Cf. Bonacina "Theol. Moral." Vol. III. in Prefix.

2 Const. "*Romanus Pontifex,*" Aug. 28, 1873; and Decree of S. Poenit. Aug. 4, 1876.

> eorumque receptores, fautores, ac generaliter quoslibet illorum defensores."

In this place we shall treat also Article III of the Constitution, since, in the new penal law, schism is assimilated to apostasy and heresy, as it was in the Bull *In Coena Domini.:*

> "Schmismaticos et eos qui a Romani Pontificis pro tempore existentis obedientia pertinaciter se subtrahunt vel recedunt."

Codex I. C. Can. 2314:

> "Omnes a christiana fide apostatae et omnes et singuli haeretici aut schismatici: incurrunt ipso facto excommunicationem. . ."

The ancient legislation of St. Paul, writing to Titus, "A man that is a heretic, after the first and second admonition, avoid, knowing that he that is such a one is subverted and sinneth, being condemned by his own judgment," [3] has inspired all subsequent anti-heretical legislation. And yet it but reproduces the still earlier teaching of Christ: "And he that will not hear the Church, let him be to thee as the heathen and the publican." [4] The Church has never departed, and will not depart, from that principle.

The article on heresy in the Const. of Pius IX, with which we are now concerned dates back to the Bulla *In Coena* of Pope Julius II, March 1, 1511, and even as far back as the Third Lateran Council (1179) there is found a formal anathema pronounced against heretics specifically and generally. Apostates are not mentioned as such until the Bulla *In Coena* of Paul V, April 8, 1610, although Boniface VIII had long since decreed that these should be treated as heretics[5], which, according to Melchior Canus[6], was done to reaffirm the custom that had long antedated

3 Tit. III 10-11.
4 Matt. xviii. 17.
5 C. 13, de heret. in VI.
6 De Locis Theol. L. 12, cap. 7.

Boniface VIII. Schism is indeed a lesser crime than heresy or apostasy, yet, because practically and historically heresy and schism nearly always go hand in hand, schism has always been severely condemned. The sentence of excommunication, however, first appears in the Bulla *In Coena* of Gregory XIII, April 14, 1583.

The Code renders untenable the opinion that the heretic does not incur the penalty unless he has joined a non-Catholic sect. For by Can. 2314, I, 3, the additional penalty of infamy is incurred by the very fact of such joining or public adherence.

Similarly, it is now beyond all question that he who positively doubts some truth of faith, i. e., who externally posits his doubt as defensible by reason (not the negative doubter who simply abstains from formulating a judgment) incurs this excommunication, for such a one must be held as a heretic, according to the definition of heresy given in the Code. (Can. 1325, 2.)

The "credentes," "receptores," "foutores" and "defensores" are not mentioned explicitly in the new law. Hence should we conclude that these do not any longer fall under the censure? Such a conclusion would be totally unwarranted. And, since this question will frequently arise in the course of the present work, we shall discuss it here and refer the subsequent cases to this discussion.

According to Can. 2231, if several persons concur to commit an offense, although only one be named in the law, those co-operators also who are considered under Can. 2209, 1-3, incur the same punishment, unless the law expressly provides otherwise. Now in Can. 2209, 1-3, there is question of those whose concurrence, physical or moral, so affects the commission of the offense that without their agency the offense would not have been committed. Hence, since the publication of the new Code, in the interpretation of these penal laws, the important thing to be known is not, as formerly, whether the co-operators are expressly named in the law as incurring the penalty; but whether those who concurred physically or morally in a given crime did so concur that without their aid or concurrence the crime would not have been committed. Once this is ascertained the rule established in Can. 2231 is easily applied. No other interpretation of the present law regarding co-operation in crime seems reasonable, especially since, in the new Code, there is hardly a mention made of co-operators in connection with any censure. Hence the provision made in Can. 2315[7] seems to apply rather to those who so believe or favor, or receive or defend, etc., that their assistance is not that of principal, but of accessory co-operators.

The censure is reserved, as heretofore, to the Holy See in a special manner. However, the declaration of the S. Cong. of the Holy Office, dated Febr. 19, 1916, is confirmed by the Code. Wherefore, the reservation obtains only in the forum of conscience. For if the offense is brought to the external forum of the Ordinary of the place in any manner, even by personal confession, the Ordinary (the Vicar General only by special mandate) can, in virtue of his ordinary power, absolve the delinquent in the external forum, provided that the absolution be preceded by an abjuration of the error made in the presence of the Ordinary, or his delegate, and at least two witnesses, and also provided that the usual penances, obligations and injunctions be placed upon the delinquent. Since absolution in the external forum has its effect also in the internal, the delinquent thus absolved from the censure by the Ordinary can be absolved from the sin itself by any confessor, the sin in itself not being reserved.

II. Const. *Apost. Sedis:*

> "Omnes et singulos scienter legentes sine auctoritate Sedis Apostolicae libros eorundem apostatarum et haereticorum haeresim propugnantes, necnon libros cujusvis auctoris per apostolicas litteras nominatim prohibitos, eosdemque libros retinentes imprimentes, et quomodolibet defendentes."

7 "Qui quoque modo haeresis propagationem sponte et scienter juvatsuspectus de haeresi est . . . . quodsi intra sex menses a contracta poena suspectus de haeresi sese non emendaverit, habeatur tanquam haereticus, haereticorum poenis obnoxius."

Codex I.C. Can. 2318, 1:

> "In excommunicationem Sedi Apostolicae speciali modo reservatam ipso facto incurrunt, opere publici facto juris, editores librorum apostatarum, haereticorum, et schismaticorum, qui apostasiam, haeresim, schisma propugnant, itemque eosdem libros aliosve per apostolicas litteras nominatim prohibitos defendentes aut scienter sine debita licentia legentes vel retinentes."

The books of heretics have always suffered the same condemnation as the authors themselves, for their books are the expression of the heretical thoughts and errors on whose account the authors have been condemned.[8] As early as 494 Pope Gelasius I, in a Roman synod, published the names of and condemned certain heretical books of the time, together with the authors themselves. This was the celebrated "Decretum Gelasianum," sometimes called the "first Roman Index."[9]

With the rapid and wide dissemination of writings consequent upon the invention of the art of printing in the fifteenth century greater precautions were required to safeguard the faith of pastors and people alike. The Council of Trent drew up its "Index librorum Prohibitorum," forbidding under pain of excommunication the publishing of any book heretical or suspected of heresy. Clement VIII,[10] Alexander VII[11] and Benedict XIV[12] issued Constitutions, in which the rules adopted by Trent were applied to the peculiar needs of the times. Latterly, Pius IX and Leo XIII manifested keen solicitude in this regard, the latter publishing two Constitutions on the subject.[13]

The present article of the Const. *Apost. Sedis* is a limitation of the Tridentine and Clementine law, and is

8 Pennachi, "Commentarium in Const. *Apost. Sedis*" I, p. 113.

9 Ibid.

10 "Cum Haebraeorum," Febr. 28, 1593.

11 "Cum ad aures," Jun. 25, 1665.

12 "Detestabilem," Nov. 10, 1752.

13 *Officiorum ac munerum*, Jan. 25, 1897; *Romani Pontifices*, Sept. 27, 1900.

derived from the Bulla *In Coena.* The law of today does not substantially depart from that of the Constitution. The Code does not mention the "imprimentes," about whom a controversy waged after the publication of the Const. of 1869.[14] Nor are the "typographi" included, who by the latest emendation of the "Index"[15] were held subject to the censure. Of all those who engage in the publication of the books in question, the only persons who are now liable to the censure are the editors, who in their own name commit to the various workmen the making of the impression[16]. Hence the typographer, as such, does not incur the penalty, but only as an editor in the strict sense. Likewise the author, who merely prepares the matter, but does not engage in the publication as an editor, is not held by the present law. The reason for this limitation is quite evident, for the criminal act by which society suffers from such books is not so much the composition of the book as the giving of the book to the public. This is also reflected in the clause inserted in Can. 2318: "opere publici juris facto," in virtue of which the censure is contracted only when the condemned book has been placed on public sale.[17]

It has been asserted[18] that Bishops, in virtue of Can. 1401, by which they are exempted from the prohibition against keeping or reading condemned books, cannot be held by the penal law contained in Can. 2318, I. This deduction seems unwarranted, for, while a bishop may not offend against this law by retaining or reading such books, he can do so in other ways, such as defending these books or assisting in their publication, and thereby incur the censure. Moreover, it may here be observed that in Can. 2227, 2, where it is declared that bishops are not comprehended under laws imposing *latae sententiae* punishments, the censure of excommunication is not included.

14 Cf. Pennachi, op. cit. II p. 230; Capello, "De Censuris" n. 76.
15 Const. *Officiorum ac munerum,* n. 47.
16 Capello, l.c.
17 Cf. Lega, "Praelectiones in Textum Jur. Can. Vol. III, n. 341.
18 Capello op. cit. n. 76.

IV. Const. *Apost. Sedis:*

> "Omnes et singulos cujuscunque status, gradus seu conditionis fuerint, ab ordinationibus seu mandatis Romanorum Pontificum pro tempore existentium ad universale futurum concilium appellantes, nec non eos quorum auxilio, consilio vel favore appellatum fuerit."

Codex I.C. Can. 2332:

> "Omnes et singuli cujuscunque status, gradus seu conditionis etiam regalis, episcopalis vel cardinalitiae fuerint, a legibus, decretis, mandatis Romani Pontificis pro tempore existentis ad Universale Concilium appellantes, sunt suspecti de haeresi et ipso facto contrahunt excommunicationem Sedi Apostolicae speciali modo reservatam."[19]

This law dates back to the pontificate of Pius II, who first enacted it by the Const. *Execrabilis*, dated Jan. 18, 1459. The true conception of papal jurisdiction had become considerably obscured in the confusion attendant upon the Great Schism of the West. Such men as Gelnhausen and Langenstein in Germany, and Gerson in France, lent their favor to the theory that a General Council is superior in authority to the Roman Pontiff.[20] The pronouncement of Pius II was a rebuke to this insidious doctrine, which was fraught with such danger that the offenders were threatened with excommunication or, in the case of a moral person, interdict. The penalty was confirmed and renewed by Julius II,[21] inserted in the *Bulla Coenae*, and finally re-enacted by Pius IX.

It has been held[22] that, since the universal primacy of jurisdiction of the Roman Pontiff was formally defined in the Council of Florence (1439) and the papal infalli-

19 Cf. Can. 1880: "Non est locus appellationi a sententia ipsius Summi Pontificis."

20 Cf. Pastor, "History of the Popes" Vol. I, p. 182 ff.

21 Const. *Suscepti regiminis,* July 1, 1539.

22 Cf. Penn. I. p. 405-406.

bility in the Vatican Council (1869), the appeal in question clearly implied heresy and schism, and, therefore, that a specific penalty of excommunication was unnecessary. However, the penalty is retained in the new Code, which declares the offenders suspected of heresy, implying thereby that the heresy in the appeal is not always evident.

The new law merely clarifies the former law. The Const. of Pius IX forbade appeals "ab ordinationibus seu mandatis." Hence some concluded that those who appealed from statutes or laws were not comprehended by the law.[23] But the object of this censure is to vindicate the supreme jurisdiction of the Supreme Pontiff, which is no less attacked by appealing from laws and statutes. So that the present law must be held to comprehend all the jurisdictional acts of the Roman Pontiff.

The phrase "ad futurum Universale Concilium" of the Const. of 1869 becomes, in the Code, "ad Universale Concilium," to obviate the interpretation made, and perhaps correctly, that the penalty was not contracted by appellants to a present council even though this be interrupted.[24]

As to the co-operators in this as in other crimes involving censures, we must refer to what has been said by way of general treatment under Article I of the present chapter.

V. Const. *Apost. Sedis:*

> "Omnes interficientes, mutilantes, percutientes, capientes, carcerantes, detinentes, vel hostiliter insequentes S.R.E. Cardinales, Patriarchas, Archiepiscopos, Episcopos, Sedisque Apostolicae Legatos, vel Nuncios, aut eos a suis dioecesibus, territoriis, terris, seu dominiis ejicientes, necnon ea mandantes, vel rata habentes seu praestantes in eis auxilium, consilium vel favorem."

23 Cf. D'Annibale, l. c. n. 47.

24 Cf. D'Annibale, "Comment. in Const. *Apost. Sedis*" n. 47. For the penalty imposed on delinquent moral persons in this matter, see Chap. VI.

Codex I.C. Can. 2343; 2:

> "Qui . . . violentas manus injecerit . . . in personam S.R.E. Cardinalis, vel Legati Romani Pontificis: 1. In excommunicationem incurrit latae sententiae Sedi Apostolicae speciali modo reservatam; 3. Qui in personam Patriarchae, Archiepiscopi, Episcopi, etiam Titularis tantum, incurrit excommunicationem latae sententiae Sedi Apostolicae speciali modo reservatam."

As heresy and schism endanger the internal life of the Church, so the violation of the hierarchy is an affront to the Church's holy and juridical constitution, and affects her external life. For he who lays violent hands upon such persons commits more than a sacrilege, since he despises the divine constitution of the Church and thereby so augments the sacrilege as to render it a public crime in the society of the Church.

In the ancient law the malicious injury of a cleric was punished by severe canonical penances, and in some cases by excommunication.[25] A person wounding a bishop incurred *ipso facto* excommunication.[26] When, about the middle of the twelfth century, at the instigation of politico-religious agitators, like Arnold of Brescia, excesses were committed against the defenceless clergy and religious, to whom the carrying of weapons was forbidden, the Church was constrained to enact more stringent measures. Thus the Second Council of Lateran (1139),[27] after the Synods of Clermont (1130), Rheims (1131) and Pisa (1135), decreed that whosoever thenceforth laid violent hands on a cleric or a monk incurred *ipso facto* anathema, the removal of which, except in danger of death, was reserved to the Roman Pontiff and must be sought in person at Rome.[28] This exemption of the clergy, which, from the opening words of the

25 C. 21, 22, 23, 24, CXVII, q. 4.
26 Synod of Rome, 862, c. XIV.
27 C. XV.
28 C. 29, C. XVII, q. 4.

Lateran canon, is called "Privilegium Canonis *'Si quis suadente diabolo,'* " or simply "Privilegium Canonis," has endured up to the present day, and is enjoyed by clerics and male and female religious alike.

The Code confirms the penal law of the Const. of Pius IX, derived from the *Bulla Coenae*. The present law, however, is more plainly and more logically stated, in accordance with the general principles: "Delictum augetur pro majore dignitate personae . . . quae delicto offenditur,"[29] and, "In poenis decernendis servetur aequa proportio cum delicto."[30] Observing these principles, the Legislator in the Code punishes violators of the "privilege of the canon" according to the grade of dignity of the persons violated. Wherefore, the excommunication under which they fall who lay violent hands on the august person of the Holy Father is reserved to him in a most special manner; moreover, the subject of this excommunication is *ipso facto vitandus,*[31] *ipso facto infamis,* and, if he be a cleric, should be degraded. (Can. 2343, 1.) This is the most severe punishment the Code prescribes for any single crime.

When the offense is committed against the person of a Cardinal, Legate, Patriarch, Archbishop or Bishop, even titular, the excommunication is reserved to the Apostolic See *speciali modo,* but in the case of the first two named infamy of law is incurred and other punishments (*ferendae sententiae*) are provided. Finally, the laying of violent hands upon a cleric or a religious of either sex likewise merits excommunication, reserved, however, only to the Ordinary of the delinquent, who may also inflict other punishments.[32]

29 Can. 2207.

30 Can. 2218, I.

31 Notwithstanding the provision of Can. 2258, 2, that no one is "vitandus" unless he has been excommunicated by name, by the Holy See, the excommunication has been publicly announced and the decree expressly declares that he is to be avoided.

32 Cf. Chapter II, Art. II.

VI. Const. *Apost. Sedis:*

"Impedientes directe vel indirecte exercitium jurisdictionis ecclesiasticae sive interni sive externi fori, et ad hoc recurrentes ad forum saeculare, eiusque mandata procurantes, edentes, aut auxilium, consilium vel favorem praestantes."

Codex I.C. Can. 2334:

"Excommunicatione latae sententiae speciali modo Sedi Apostolicae reservata plectuntur: . . . Qui impediunt directe vel indirecte exercitium jurisdictionis ecclesiasticae sive interni sive externi fori, ad hoc recurrentes ad quamlibet laicalem potestatem."

The purpose of the present censure is to protect the jurisdiction which the Church, as a perfect and independent society, ordained to govern the Christian people, enjoys.[33] Ecclesiastical jurisdiction, insofar as it covers the relations of man to God, is called "jurisdiction of the internal forum," which is further distinguished into "Sacramental" and "non-sacramental," according as it is exercised inside or outside the tribunal of Penance. "Jurisdiction of the external forum" is that which regulates the external ecclesiastical relations.

The exercise of ecclesiastical jurisdiction is hindered by denying to the Church the essentials of jurisdiction itself, by obstructing the issuance of mandates, and by recalling mandates already awaiting execution. The present censure, the 16th in the *Bulla Coenae,* was inserted therein by Pius V in 1570, and extended by Pius IX so as to embrace the internal as well as the external forum, and delegated as well as ordinary power.

In the new law there is no material departure from the Constitution of 1869 in this regard. Two changes have been made in the wording of the law, apparently to correct the interpretation that was generally adopted by commentators.[34] From the particle "et" in the clause

33 Decr. *Lamentabili sane,* July 3, 1907, n. 52 ff.

34 Cf. Pennacchi, op. cit. II. p. 11; D'Annibale, op. cit. n. 61; Avanzini, "De Const. Apost. Sedis," n. 7; Lega, op. cit. n. 442.

"et ad hoc recurrentes, etc.," it was inferred that another species of persons, distinct from the "impedientes," was intended by the Legislator, the particle "et" being equivalent to the disjunctive "vel." The omission of the particle from the newly promulgated law would indicate that the recourse is a necessary condition to incurring the penalty, so that one who hinders ecclesiastical jurisdiction without having recourse to the lay power cannot be said to contract the present censure.[35]

The other question centered upon the phrase "ad forum saeculare." D'Annibale[36] held that since these words were to be taken according to their acceptation in civil law, and therefore signified a judicial forum, the censure was not to be incurred by a person who had recourse not to a judge, but to a Prefect, Magistrate, etc. The interpretation offered by Card. Lega[37] has prevailed in the Code. He pointed out that "forum saeculare" was used, in this case, in contradistinction to the ecclesiastical forum taken in its widest sense, and hence should be understood to comprehend every species of lay magistracy. This opinion is confirmed by the wording of Canon 2334: "ad quamlibet laicalem potestatem."

VII. Const. *Apost. Sedis:*

> **"Cogentes sive directe sive indirecte judices laicos ad trahendum ad suum tribunal personas ecclesiasticas praeter canonicas dispositiones; item edentes leges vel decreta contra libertatem aut jura Ecclesiae."**

Codex I.C., Can. 2341:

> **"Si quis contra praescriptum can. 120 ausus fuerit ad judicem laicum trahere aliquem ex S.R.E. Cardinalibus vel Legatis Sedis Apostolicae, vel Officialibus Majoribus Romanae Curiae ob negotia ad eorum munus pertinentia, vel Ordinarium proprium, contrahit ipso facto excommunicationem**

35 Cf. Sole, l. c. n. 360.
36 Loc. cit.
37 Loc. cit.

Sedi Apostolicae speciali modo reservatam; si alium episcopum etiam mere titularem, aut Abbatem vel Praelatum nullius, vel aliquem ex supremis religionum juris pontificii Superioribus, excommunicationem latae sententiae Sedi Apostolicae simpliciter reservatam; demum si, non obtenta ab Ordinario loci licentia, aliam personam privilegio fori fruentem, clericus quidem incurrit ipso facto in suspensionem ab officio reservatam Ordinario, laicus autem congruis poenis pro gravitate culpae a proprio Ordinario puniatur."

Can. 2334:

"Excommunicatione latae sententiae speciali modo Sedi Apostolicae reservata plectuuntur: Qui leges, mandata, vel decreta contra libertatem aut jura Ecclesiae edunt . . ."

In the first part of the present article the Legislator protects the "privilegium fori," whereby the clergy are entitled to a special tribunal in criminal and contentious causes, before an ecclesiastical judge. By their nature the civil causes of clerics pertain as much to the lay courts as do those of the laity; but it is incongruous that those who are the fathers and teachers of the laity should be judged by the laity. Moreover, it is a matter of history that many laics were inclined to oppress the clergy and found the courts a favorable occasion for actual oppression.[38] So that the Church was constrained to withdraw her servants, even in civil matters, from the lay courts and place them exclusively under ecclesiastical jurisdiction.[39]

The principle, that no cleric should be summoned before the lay courts, was called into life by the medieval popes and, by decretal law, the exclusive competence of ecclesiastical judges over clerics in civil and in criminal causes was established.[40] In the Councils of Chalcedon (451) and Toledo (589) excommunication was threat-

38 C. 3, de Immun. in Sexto, III, 23.

39 Cf. Penn. I, 259, ff.

40 Cc. 4, 8, 10, 17, X, de jud. II, 1; Cc. 1, 2, 9, 12, 13, X, de foro compet., II, 2.

ened upon any cleric who would sue another cleric before a secular tribunal, which penalty was extended to the laity by the Councils of Cologne (1226), Exeter (1287), Leyde (1293) and others. This legislation was chiefly local, but with the multiplication of the abuses in the fourteenth and fifteenth centuries Pope Martin V, in the Const. "Ad reprimendas insolentias," Feb. 1, 1428, extended the censure to the Universal Church, and decreed that all persons, secular, cleric or religious, judges and their accomplices, private persons as well as those in authority, who would summon clerics before lay tribunals, or take an active and leading part in the proceedings against them, would suffer the penalty of excommunication.

In the *Bulla Coenae*, which, for a long period, represents the discipline of the Church, and from which the present article of the Constitution was drawn, the excommunication was decreed against legislators who enact laws contrary to the rights of the Church, and against public officials who bring into their tribunals physical or moral ecclesiastical persons who enjoy the privilege of the forum. It was seen, however, that, if the judges themselves remained under the threat of censure, the way would be closed for Catholics to assume such places and purify and moderate the lay tribunals, leaving the offices to be filled by weak and irreligious men who would stop at no excess. Wisely then, did Pius IX mitigate the law, exempting the judges from the censure and binding only those who force the judge, directly or indirectly, to summon ecclesiastical persons.[41] This class and those who publish laws contrary to the liberty and rights of the Church were the only ones held by the law of Pius IX.

The Congregation of the Holy Office, in a decree approved by Leo XIII Jan. 23, 1886, declared that private persons who sue clerics before lay tribunals were not comprehended among the "cogentes," yet those persons should have at least the authorization of their Ordinary,

41 Cf. Decr. of S. Office, June 15, 1870, Feb. 1, 1871.

or of the Pope for the suing of a bishop, and the violators of this rule were liable to punishment.

Greater severity marked the modification of this legislation by Pius X, who decreed[42] that excommunication *latae sententiae* and specially reserved to the Roman Pontiff, is incurred by all private persons, lay or clerical, male or female, who, without permission of the ecclesiastical authority, call before lay judges any ecclesiastical persons and compel them to appear publicly in court, either in criminal or in civil causes.

The Code maintains the principle of the "Privilege of the forum." Clerics in civil, or, as the terminology of the Code has it, *contentious* cases as well as in *criminal* cases, are to be tried only by ecclesiastical judges, unless permission has been obtained to bring them to the lay court, or some provision has been legitimately made, as for example, by concordats, formal concessions, etc.

We have seen that, under the discipline of the *Bulla Coenae*, the penalty was incurred not by private persons but by the judges or officials; under the Const. *Apost. Sedis*, not by the "trahentes" and judges, but by legislators and higher officials, or the "cogentes," who freely and "a nullis coacti" forced the judge to summon; and finally, under the Motu Proprio "Quantavis diligentia," by private persons also, who brought suit in the lay courts. In the new law the lawmakers[43] and the "trahentes" [44] are both held subject to the censure. In the former case the old law is confirmed and its interpretation therefore prevails. The word "mandata" has been inserted so as to allow no cause for the exemption of those who legislate contrary to the liberty and rights of the Church in single cases or with respect to individuals. Both judges and plaintiffs may be "trahentes," although in practice the judge will seldom be affected since presumption and full malice are required,[45] and he is

42 Motu Proprio "Quantavis diligentia," Oct. 9, 1911.

43 Can. 2334, 1.

44 Can. 2341.

45 Can. 2229, 2.

generally considered as compelled by his superiors to act when suit has been brought by a plaintiff.

As to the penalties themselves, the general principle of proportion between the penalty and the dignity of the person offended is applied in the newly promulgated law. Thus the excommunication incurred by suing a Cardinal, Legate of the Holy See, or major Official in matters that pertain to their respective offices, or even one's own Ordinary, is reserved to the Holy See *speciali modo;* while in the case of any other bishop, Abbot or Prelate *nullius*, or Supreme Superior of a pontifical religion is reserved only *simpliciter*. Finally, the suing, without permission, of any lesser person who enjoys the "privilege of the forum" brings upon an offending cleric suspension from office reserved to the Ordinary, but laics now incur no penalty *latae sententiae*, their punishment being left to the judgment of their respective Ordinaries.

VIII. Const. *Apost. Sedis:*

> "Recurrentes ad laicam potestatem ad impediendas litteras vel acta quaelibet a Sede Apostolica, vel ab ejusdem Legatis aut Delegatis quibuscumque profecta, eorumque promulgationem vel exsecutionem directe vel indirecte prohibentes, aut eorum causa sive ipsas partes, sive alios laedentes vel perterrefacientes."

Codex I.C., Can. 2333:

> "Recurrentes ad laicam potestatem ad impediendas litteras vel acta quaelibet a Sede Apostolica vel ab ejusdem Legatis profecta, eorumve promulgationem vel exsecutionem directe vel indirecte prohibentes, aut eorum causa sive eos ad quos pertinent litterae vel acta sive alios laedentes vel perterrefacientes, ipso facto subjaceant excommunicationi Sedi Apostolicae speciali modo reservatae."

The exercise of any power is completed by the execution of the laws, mandates and decrees through which that power functions. If these cannot be made effective the power is vain. The laws and decrees of the Church are generally promulgated, directly or indirectly, by documents, of which there are several species, so that if these are not permitted to reach their proper destinations the exercise of the jurisdiction of the Church is in so far impeded. This constitutes so serious an injury as to merit the severe penalty of excommunication.

This pernicious interference has many times beset the Church in the exercise of her legitimate power and has been duly punished with excommunication. In the time of Boniface IX (1389-1404) the abuse had become so prevalent that he issued a decree against it, which decree is cited by Leo X (1513-1521), although it is not found in the "Bullarium." In 1418 Martin V[46] recalled the concessions which Urban VI had granted to certain prelates, whereby Letters Apostolic might not be promulgated until presented to those Prelates or their Officials. Subsequently, Julius II,[47] Leo X,[48] and Clement VII[49] were constrained to prevent certain prelates who, under the pretext of avoiding frauds, required that no Pontifical document could have effect in their respective territories until they had been submitted to these prelates. Some even appealed to the secular powers for the support of their claims. All these abuses were condemned and punished in the Bulla Coenae, from which the present article of the Constitution is derived.

As the former discipline in this matter is continued "ex integro" in the new law, and is therefore to be interpreted as heretofore, it is beyond the province of this work to discuss the law at length. It is noticed, however, that the phrase "aut delegatis quibuscumque" of the Const. of Pius IX is omitted in the Code. This effects no change in the law since "legati" is used in the Code in a generic sense so as to comprehend not only Apostolic Delegates but also nuncios and internuncios. (Can. 267.)

46 Const. *Quod antidota,* Apr. 30, 1418.

47 Const. *Consueverunt,* Mar. 1, 1511.

48 Loc. cit.

49 Const. *Romanus Pontifex,* Dec. 29, 1533.

IX. Const. *Apost. Sedis:*

> "Omnes falsarios litterarum Apostolicarum, etiam in forma Brevis ac supplicationum gratiam vel iustitiam concernentium, per Romanum Pontificem, vel S.R.E. Vice-Cancellarios seu Gerentes vices eorum aut de mandato ejusdem Romani Pontificis signatarum; necnon falso publicantes Litteras Apostolicas, etiam in forma Brevis, et etiam falso signantes supplicationes hujusmodi sub nomine Romani Pontificis seu Vice-Cancellarii aut Gerentis vices praedictorum."

Codex I.C., Can. 2360:

> "Omnes fabricatores vel falsarii litterarum, decretorum vel rescriptorum Sedis Apostolicae vel iisdem litteris decretis vel rescriptis scienter utentes incurrunt ipso facto in excommunicationem speciali modo Sedi Apostolicae reservatam."

The Const. *Apost. Sedis* next concerns itself with the crime of falsehood ("crimen falsi"), or the changing or suppression of the truth to the detriment of another, or to one's own gain.[50]

The falsification of ecclesiastical, and particularly Pontifical, documents has given rise to serious evils, both public and private. Precautions have always been taken to prevent such crimes. In the middle ages, when the transmission of documents afforded more facility for falsification than it does today, the Popes and the Councils had frequent occasions to reprobate and condemn the crime of falsehood.[51] The legislation of these pontiffs was partly retained in the *Bulla Coenae,* in which the present excommunication is the sixth one named.

In the very early publications of the *Bulla Coenae* the censure is inflicted upon the "falso fabricatores." This, however, was changed by Pope Alexander VII to read "falso publicantes, etc.," probably on the conviction that "fabricated" letters would not be productive of the evil

50 Wernz, "Jus Decretalium" VI, n. 421, ss; D'Annibale, op. cit. n. 78.

51 C. 5, 7, X, de crimine falsi, V. 20.

effects if they were not published, just as, in the case of books of heretics and apostates, the editors, and not the authors as such, are punished with the censure. Pennachi points out that this was not a happy change, since ignorance might frequently excuse the publishers from the penalty, whereas the "fabricatores" could not resort to the plea so easily.[52]

The Const. *Apost. Sedis* retained the class of "publicantes," but the Code replaces it with the class originally punished—the "fabricatores," although authorities were not wanting who held that these were already comprehended among the "falsarios" of the Constitution.[53]

The question of using falsified or fictitious letters Apostolic, etc., will be treated in Chapter III, in accordance with the order followed in the Const. *Apostolicae Sedis.*

X. Const. *Apost. Sedis:*

> "Absolventes complicem in peccato turpi etiam in mortis articulo, si alius sacerdos, licet non approbatus ad confessiones, sine gravi aliqua exoritura infamia et scandalo, possit excipere morientis confessionem."

Codex I.C., Can. 2367:

> 1. "Absolvens vel fingens absolvere complicem in peccato turpi incurrit ipso facto in excommunicationem specialissimo modo Sedi Apostolicae reservatam; idque etiam in mortis articulo, si alius sacerdos, licet non approbatus ad confessiones, sine gravi aliqua exoritura infamia et scandalo, possit excipere morientis confessionem, excepto casu quo moribundus recuset alii confiteri.
>
> 2. Eandem excommunicationem non effugit absolvens vel fingens absolvere complicem qui peccatum quidem complicitatis, a quo nondum est absolutus, non confitetur, sed ideo ita se gerit, quia ad id a complice confessario sive directe sive indirecte inductus est."

That a confessor who has been a party to the committing of a sin should absolve his accomplice from that sin

52 Op. cit. I. p. 302.
53 Cf. D'Annibale, op. cit. n. 81; Pennachi, l. c.

is contrary to the spirit in which the Sacred tribunal of Penance was established, and, if permitted, would, as the history of the question testifies, offer occasion for repetition of the sin. With regard to sins *contra sextum* this is especially true. Wherefore the Church, zealous for the sanctity of the sacrament of Penance, and manifesting her vehement condemnation of any abuse in its administration, forbids a confessor, under pain of the most severe punishments, to absolve or feign the absolution of his accomplice in *peccato turpi.*

The first general legislation in this matter was the Const. "Sacramentum Poenitentiae" of Benedict XIV, published June 1, 1741, and confirmed and renewed by that pontiff[54] as well as by Pius IX in the article now under consideration. By subsequent decrees the law has been completed and officially interpreted, and thus perfected it comes to us in the new Code. Thus the confessor who feigns absolution is included under the law, in accordance with the response given by the S. Poenitentiary Mar. 1, 1878,[55] and confirmed by the Holy Office Dec. 5, 1883. The very words of a response of the S. Poenitentiary[56] are inserted in the new law, in virtue of which the excommunication is likewise incurred by the confessor simulating or attempting the absolution of his accomplice, who does not confess the sin *contra sextum* because the confessor has, either directly or indirectly, induced the penitent to omit the mention of that sin.

A certain exception to the law, which has found favor with many theologians, has now been inserted in the law. In virtue of this the confessor can, in case of danger of death, hear the confession of and absolve his accomplice whose salvation is placed in hazard either because

54 Const. *Apostolic muneris*, Feb. 8, 1745; Const. *Inter praeteritos*, Dec. 3, 1749. The Const. *Sacr. Poenit* has been made part of the new Code, being the fifth of the eight Constitutions appended to the Canons.

55 Confessarios simulantes absolutionem complicis in peccato turpi non effugere excommunicationem reservatam in Const. Bened. XIV *Sacram. Poenit.*

56 Feb. 19, 1896.

the penitent refuses to confess to any other confessor or would thereby make a sacrilegious confession. The salvation of a soul is then at stake and in that case the Church wisely departs from an otherwise stringent rule.

Finally, it will be seen that the new law expressly reserves the absolution from this censure to the Holy See *specialissimo modo*. This is one of the four censures thus reserved by the new Code. However, even before the promulgation of the Code this excommunication was considered to be reserved *specialissimo modo*, as is seen from the decrees of the Holy Office[57] in which it was declared that this case, as contained in the Const. "Sacramentum Poenitentiae" was thenceforth excluded even from the very extensive faculties granted to bishops and missionaries.

XI. Const. *Apost. Sedis:*

> "Usurpantes aut sequestrantes jurisdictionem, bona, reditus, ad personas ecclesiasticas ratione suarum ecclesiarum aut beneficiorum pertinentes."

Codex I.C., Can. 2346:

> "Si quis bona ecclesiastica cujuslibet generis, sive mobilia, sive immobilia, sive corporalia, sive incorporalia, per se vel per alios in proprios usus convertere et usurpare praesumpserit aut impedire ne eorundem fructus seu reditus ab iis, ad quos jure pertinent, percipiantur, excommunicationi tandiu subiaceat, quandiu bona ipsa integre restituerit, praedictum impedimentum removerit ac deinde a Sede Apostolica absolutionem impetraverit."

The Church, from the beginning, has possessed and consistently vindicated the right to possess certain temporal goods whereby her ministers, given over to the higher and spiritual things, might be sustained, the poor relieved and the means of divine worship assured. Accordingly she has not hesitated to impose her most severe punishments upon those who would usurp such goods.

57 Jan. 27, 1866 and Apr. 4, 1871.

Thus in the fifth National Council of Orleans (549)[58] the usurpers of ecclesiastical goods were condemned as "murderers of the poor"; the Fathers of the Council of Melde (845), confirming the decree of the Council of Orleans, obliged a bishop to restore certain ecclesiastical goods that had been alienated and to prohibit any further depredations.[59] The Council of Tours (1163) decreed punishment of those bishops and clerics who had conceded to laics tithes and other goods belonging to the Church.

Mindful of the ancient discipline, the Fathers of the Council of Trent[60] decreed the penalty of excommunication against usurpers of the goods of the Church and pious places.[61] The Tridentine decree left no one exempt from its observance, neither king, prince, laic nor ecclesiastic. The rights of the Church in this regard had to be evinced forcibly. And so the censure against usurpers quite naturally was included in the *Bulla Coenae.*[62]

The present article of the Const. *Apost. Sedis* was taken from the said Bull, but is not a literal reproduction of it. There is no mention of "bona" in the *Bulla Coenae,* while the Constitution expressly mentioned "usurpantes bona"; the former speaks of "jurisdictions," the latter of "jurisdiction"; the former includes "monasteries" within its law, while the latter omits that class and protects the ecclesiastical goods of "Churches and Benefices." However, the despoilers of monasteries would fall under the Tridentine censure. Today, with the comprehensive

58 Can. xiii.

59 Can. xvii.

60 Sess. xxii, cap. 11, de ref.

61 This penalty is excommunication reserved "simpliciter" to the Holy See, but it is deemed more opportune to consider it here together with that contained in the Const. of 1869, since by the new Code all ecclesiastical goods, according to the definition of the same contained in Can. 1497, are defended by one censure (Can. 2346), namely excommunication reserved *speciali modo* to the Holy See.

62 No. xvii.

definition of "bona ecclesiastica" as given in Can. 1497,[63] the usurpation of such goods or any part of them is penalized with excommunication incurred *ipso facto* and specially reserved to the Holy See. Clerical and lay persons are alike liable to the censure, and even regulars, whom the law formerly did not comprehend.[64]

Since the new law retains the clause, "in proprios usus convertere et usurpare," it is pertinent to add that not every conversion of ecclesiastical goods into private use is punished with the censure, but only that which is done authoritatively, when the usurper pretends to be using his rights or making use of goods to which he has a just claim. This interpretation conforms with the decree of the Holy Office[65] in which it was declared that the censure is not incurred by thieves, plunderers, etc., who make no pretence of possessing a right to these goods.

The pre-requisite to absolution which the Council of Trent established in this case is confirmed in the new law; i.e., the goods usurped must have been restored in their entirety, and any impediment to their enjoyment or use must have been removed. Now it is a general rule that absolution from a censure cannot be denied once the delinquent has desisted from his contumacy and has made congruous satisfaction for any loss or scandal that has resulted from his offence, or has seriously promised to make such satisfaction. Canon 2346 declares what satisfaction is congruous in the present case and is therefore required before absolution can be obtained.

XII. Const. *Apost. Sedis:*

> "Invadentes, destruentes, detinentes per se vel per alios Civitates, Terras, loca aut jura ad Ecclesiam Romanam pertinentia; vel usurpantes, perturbantes, retinentes supremam jurisdictionem in

63 "Bona temporalia, sive corporalia, tum immobilia tum mobilia, sive incorporalia, quae vel ad Ecclesiam universam et ad Apostolicam Sedem vel ad aliam in Ecclesia personam moralem pertineant, sunt bona ecclesiastica."

64 Cf. Capello, op. cit. n. 116; Cerato, "Censurae Vigentes," n. 84.

65 Mar. 9, 1870.

> eis; necnon ad singula praedicta auxilium, consilium, favorem praebentes."

Codex I.C., Can. 2345:

> "Usurpantes vel detinentes per se vel per alios bona aut jura ad Ecclesiam Romanam pertinentia, subjaceant excommunicationi latae sententiae speciali modo Sedi Apostolicae reservatae; . . ."

By this censure the Legislator intends to defend the temporal possessions of the Holy See. The Church is a society, existing for the sake of men and carrying on her high work among men, for which she needs, and therefore has the right to, the use of temporal goods. Nevertheless her right of temporal dominion has for many years been assailed; false rights have been asserted to wrest it from her, and men have not hesitated to resort to the use of arms.[66]

The temporal dominion of the Popes began with the natural and gradual acquisition of landed property, from the time of Gregory the Great onward, which in those days carried with it princely authority over the tenants and inhabitants of the estates. A desire for self-government gradually took hold of the Italians and they began to look to the Bishop of Rome as their natural Ruler, their defender and protector against all foreign power. It is a matter of history how the Pope, with the assistance of Pepin, became an independent Sovereign, ruling over the states that had been presented to the "Apostolic See" as the "patrimony of St. Peter," not belonging to any Pope as an individual, nor to any family or faction, but to the Universal Church.[67]

It was to prevent the invasion and molestation of these lands that the penalty now under discussion was inserted in the *Bulla Coenae*[68] and renewed annually after the established custom. Pius IX, in the revision of the censure law, confirmed the article of the *Bulla* in its en-

66 Cf. Cath. Enc. s. v. "Ecclesiastical Property."

67 Birkhauser, "History of the Catholic Church," p. 283 ff.

68 No. xx.

tirety, without, however, specifying the different lands and places affected, as was done in the *Bulla Coenae*. He forbade the invasion, destruction, and detention of the "cities, lands, places and rights" which belonged to the Roman Church, the rights being of course those peculiar to princes. The law of today protects, besides these rights, the "goods" belonging to the Roman Church, resting upon the definition of ecclesiastical goods as given in Can. 1497.

The acts of invading, destroying, and perturbing are not mentioned in the Code, so that these, unless they amount to usurpation or detention, do not any longer fall under the law. And while the usurpers and detainers are specifically mentioned in the new law, yet it cannot be doubted that the principal co-operators[69] are also liable to the censure. The present law, therefore, is substantially a confirmation of the traditional censure against the invaders of the Papal States.

The preceding twelve censures comprise the list of excommunications reserved *speciali modo* to the Apostolic See which remained in force after the promulgation of the Constitution *Apostolicae Sedis*. Subsequently, however, two more excommunications, likewise reserved, were enacted, one in the Const. *Romanus Pontifex*, Aug. 28, 1873, and one by the S. Penitentiary, Aug. 4, 1876. Moreover, with the promulgation of the Code of 1918 four new censures of excommunication, which require mention in this place, come into existence. Of these two are reserved *speciali modo* and two *specialissimo modo* to the Apostolic See. These we shall now treat in the order in which they were enacted.

XIII. Const. *Romanus Pontifex* Aug. 28, 1873:

> "Si dignitates, Canonici cathedrales . . . concedere et transferre in nominatum et praesentatum ad eamdem ecclesiam, eius curam, regimen et administrationem . . . ausi fuerint, praeter

69 Cann. 2207, 2231.

> nullitatem . . . praedictae concessionis et translationis, praefatos Canonicos et Dignitates excommunicationis majoris, necnon privationis fructuum ecclesiasticorum beneficiorum quorumcumque, aliorum redituum ecclesiasticorum per eos respective obtentorum, similiter eo ipso incurrendis poenis innodamus, et innodatos fore decernimus et declaramus; ipsarumque poenarum absolutionem seu relaxationem Nobis et Romano Pontifici pro tempore existenti dumtaxat specialiter reservamus.
>
> "In easdem poenas pariter reservatas ipso facto incurrunt nominati et praesentati ad vacantes ecclesias, qui earum curam, regimen et administrationem suscipere audeant ex concessione et translatione a Dignitatibus et Canonicis aliisque de quibus supra, in eos peracta; necnon ii, qui praemissis paruerint, vel auxilium, consilium aut favorem praestiterint, cujuscunque status, conditionis et praeeminentiae et dignitatis fuerint."

This censure, as is seen from the Constitution itself, was directed first, against the dignitaries and Canons of cathedral churches, or those having the administration of vacant cathedrals, who would dare to concede and transfer the administration of their Church to the person elected by the Chapter or named or presented to the said Church by a lay power; secondly, against those so elected or presented and unlawfully admitted; and thirdly, against those who would obey the illegitimate superior or aid, advise or assist, in any way, the aforesaid offenders.

The traditional discipline of the Church in the matter of providing for vacant sees is represented by the well-known rule: "No benefice can be lawfully obtained without canonical institution," [70] the latter being the concession of the benefice by competent ecclesiastical authority. As early as 592 Pope Gregory the Great admonished the Bishop John that the see of Scylla was not absolutely conceded to him but only entrusted to him during his exile

70 Reg. Jur. n. 1, in Sexto.

from his proper see.[71] Gregory VII, in the Synod of Rome (1080), forbade, under pain of excommunication, the acceptance of bishoprics and abbacies at the hands of laymen.[72] Paschal II, in 1107, pronounced excommunication upon the cleric, abbot or monk who would obtain the administration of a church through the laity.[73] The presentation of apostolic letters was required by Boniface VIII, who forbade, under pain of nullity and suspension from benefice, Cathedral Chapters and Convents to admit any bishop, prelate or abbot until he had presented the required letters.[74]

And down to the present time the ecclesiastical discipline has required that the Apostolic Letters of election be presented to the Chapter, or Vicar Capitular, or Administrator, as the case may be, before possession of the benefice may be claimed by the newly elected or nominated person.[75] Pius IX, in the Const. *Romanus Pontifex*, enacted more severe penalties for the dignitaries and cathedral canons who contravene this law. Besides privation of the fruits of their benefices or other Church goods, they incurred excommunication, as above stated.

The law requiring formal presentation of the Letters Apostolic is confirmed in the new Code, which prescribes that the act of taking juridical possession of a see be performed in the Cathedral Chapter. In our country this means that the Diocesan Consultors, who take the place of the Chapter in so far as the Chapter is the senate of the bishop, must meet to receive and inspect the papal document in which the appointment is declared. However, the excommunication imposed by Pius IX no longer obtains, since it is not mentioned in the Code. (Can. 6, n. 5.) Henceforth Chapters, communities or other persons who admit anyone to a benefice, office or dignity in the Church before he has presented letters of confirmation, incur *ipso facto* the vindictive penalty of suspension

71 C. 42, C. VII, q. 1.
72 C. 12, c. XVI, q. 7.
73 C. 16, c. XVI, q. 7.
74 C. 1, de elect. I. 3, in extravag. com.
75 Cf. Can. 334, 3.

"ad beneplacitum Sanctae Sedis," from all right of election, presentation or nomination. The unlawful admission is, as formerly, null and void; the persons admitted are *ipso jure* ineligible for the benefice or office and are liable to further punishment at the hands of the Ordinary. (Can. 2394.)

XIV. The second of the excommunications inflicted since the publication of the Const. *Apost. Sedis* was that contained in the Response of the Sacred Penitentiary, dated Aug. 4, 1876.

Participation of the laity in the election of the Supreme Pontiff had long been forbidden. Following the intrusion of Constantine into the Roman See by his brother Toto of Nepi in June, 767, the Council of the Lateran[76] forbade a layman to be elected Pope or to take part in the papal elections.[77] From the time of the restoration of the Roman Empire under Otto I down to the reign of Henry IV the imperial prerogatives of nomination increased so greatly that canonical election was very much reduced in practice. And while the Emperors generally chose worthy subjects and prevented greater abuses, their extensive power constituted no small danger to the interests of the Church. Wisely, then, did Pope Nicholas II, in 1059,[78] minimize the imperial privileges in this respect, reserving the principal part in papal elections to Cardinal bishops.[79] New abuses were encountered and duly condemned by Gregory XV[80] and Urban VIII.[81]

In 1876 the question was brought before the Sacred Penitentiary in the form of a *dubium*. A publication was being circulated in Rome, showing forth the program of a newly organized society, by which the faithful

76 767.

77 C. 3, 4, 5, D. LXXIX.

78 Council of Lateran.

79 C. 1, D. 23.

80 Const. *Aeterni Patris*, Nov. 15, 1621.

81 Const. *Ad Romani Pontificis*, Jan. 28, 1626; Wernz o. c. II n. 567 ff.

were exhorted to join the said society so that, when the Holy See should become vacant, they might participate in the election of the successor. The organization was known as "The Italian Catholic Society for the Vindication of the Rights of the Christian People, and especially of the Roman People, in the Election of the Supreme Pontiff." Those who joined the society were obliged to promise, before two witnesses, to extend the society and to propagate its doctrine. Confessors sought the advice of the Sacred Penitentiary in the matter of absolving penitents who had joined the society. The substance of the Response, which was approved by Pope Pius IX, was that excommunication reserved specially to the Holy See, was *ipso facto* incurred by those who joined, promoted, favored or adhered to the said society.

This censure was enacted to meet a need peculiar to the time. Accordingly, with the cessation of activity of the "Italian Catholic Society" and the removal of the particular danger it afforded, the censure of excommunication imposed by the S. Penitentiary has been abrogated by its omission from the new Code, which provides that the present discipline in the matter of papal elections is to be found in the Const. *Vacante Sede Apostolica* of Pius X, promulgated Dec. 25, 1904, and appended to the canons of the Code.[82]

XV. Codex I.C., Can. 2320:

> "Qui species consecratas abiecerit vel ad malum finem abduxerit aut retinuerit, est suspectus de haeresi; incurrit in excommunicationem latae sententiae specialissimo modo Sedi Apostolicae reservatam; est ipso facto infamis, et clericus praeterea est deponendus."

This censure, which appears for the first time in the Code of 1918, is based upon the dogma of the reality and the permanence of the Presence of Our Lord Jesus Christ in the Holy Eucharist. Concomitant with the belief in this truth, which extends back to the time of Christ, have

82 Cann. 160, 2330; Wernz, op. cit. II, n. 574.

been the reverence and adoration of the Sacred Species on the part of believers. It is not strange, then, that the Church has always demanded of her children the deepest reverence for the Most August Sacrament and decried any departure from her pious traditions.[83]

In the new Code the first penalty we find for crimes against religion is the present excommunication. Three classes of persons are embraced by the censure: (a) Those who "throw away" the Sacred Species, i.e., in contempt for the Sacrament, whether actuated by impiety or incredulity, as, for example, one who breaks into the tabernacle, takes the ciborium and scatters the Sacred Particles about; not, however, one who would, for example, steal a ciborium or pyx, but leave the particles in the tabernacle or on the altar-table, for this penalty is established to protect the Sacred Species, not the utensils, from gross insult. (b) Those who remove the Sacred Species for an evil purpose; i.e., who take them from a place where they are legitimately kept and carry them elsewhere with the intention of using them unbecomingly or with the knowledge that such use will be made of them. Thus the censure would be incurred by one who steals a particle, or even receives it sacramentally and afterwards removes it from his mouth, and carries it away to be used for magic or other superstitious purposes. It matters not whether he acts gratis or for a reward. (c) Those who, although they have not taken the Sacred Species from their proper place, yet retain, for an evil purpose, Species already taken by another, whether the Species are kept openly or secretly, at home or elsewhere. The censure is incurred by him who prevents their return to the proper custody. The Sacred Species may be those of Bread or Wine, so long as they are validly consecrated according to any liturgical rite.

It is not clear from Can. 2320 whether one or two censures would be incurred when the same person takes

83 Council of Trent, Sess. xiii, Pope Hadrian VI. Ep. *Dudum* Jul. 20, 1522; Innoc. XI. Const. *Ad nostri apostalatus*, Mar. 12, 1677; Bened. XIV Const. *Ab Augustissimo*, Mar. 5, 1744; Clem. XIII Const. *Gravissimum*, Mar. 6, 1759, n. 6.

and keeps the Sacred Species for an evil purpose. Cerato,[84] applying Canon 2244, concludes that two distinct censures are thus incurred. However, we must bear in mind that this censure is not imposed on account of the "abduction" or the "retention" as such, but on account of the abduction or the retention *for an evil purpose*, which cannot be accomplished unless the Species are retained. Wherefore, it seems that, although two censures would be incurred if the *retinens* is distinct from the *abducens*, yet if one and the same person perform both acts he incurs only one censure.

XVI. Codex I.C., Can. 2369:

> "Confessarium, qui sigillum sacramentale directe violare praesumpserit, manet excommunicatio specialissimo modo Sedi Apostolicae reservata; . . ."

The earliest penalty recorded for the violation of the Seal of Confession is that imposed by Pope Gregory VII (1073-1085), which provided that the offending priest should be "deposed and made a life-long, ignominious wanderer."[85] Innocent III, in the fourth Lateran Council (1215), promulgating the law of annual confession, confirmed this penalty of deposition and required further that the confessor enter a monastery and do perpetual penance.[86] The execution of these punishments was again urged upon bishops in the Decree of the S. Congr. de Prop. Fide, dated April 13, 1807.[87]

Today, for the first time, we have the sacred seal of confession protected by a censure—one of the four censures which the Holy See reserves to itself *specialissimo modo*. The present law cannot be said to have been required by any disorders on the part of confessors, peculiar to our time. Indeed, the examples in history of the violation of this sacred seal are notoriously few, and are

84 "Censurae Vigentes" n. 103.
85 C. 2, D. VI, de Poenit.
86 C. 12, X, de Poenit. V. 38.
87 N. xvii.

almost nil in modern times. Rather, the Church desires, in enacting the new law, to reaffirm the sacredness of the Sacramental Secret, to proclaim to men her firm purpose to maintain that Secret inviolable,[88] and thus to protest against the action of civil magistrates who, in some instances, have claimed the right to exact from confessors testimony in matters pertaining to their sacred ministry.[89]

The censure is incurred only when the Secret is violated directly, i.e., when the matter confessed is explicitly disclosed and the person of the penitent clearly designated.[90] Moreover, the law requires presumption, so that the violation of the Seal must be made with full knowledge and deliberation, and any diminution of imputability on the part of the intellect or of the will excuses the delinquent from this excommunication, as from any other penalty *latae sententiae* contained in a law which has such words as "praesumpserit," "scienter," etc.

XVII. Codex I.C., Can. 2322:

> "Ad ordinem sacerdotalem non promotus: 1. Si Missae celebrationem simulaverit aut sacramentalem confessionem exceperit, excommunicationem ipso facto contrahit, speciali modo Sedi Apostolicae reservatam; . . ."

In the Decretals of Gregory IX we read: "Si quis baptizaverit, aut aliquod divinum officium exercuerit, non ordinatus, propter temeritatem abjiciatur ab Ecclesia, et nunquam ordinetur." [91] In other words, the usurpation of an order that had not been conferred was punished

88 Cf. Cann. 889.

89 Cf. Cath. Enc., s. v. "Seal of Confession."

90 Wernz, op. cit. VI. n. 463; Ojetti, *Synopsis Rerum Moralium* n. 3721. Note: The Holy Office on June 9, 1915, sent an Instruction to Local Ordinaries and Superiors of Religions, in which it condemned the practice of confessors who, while avoiding the mention of anything by which the penitent might become known, yet do not hesitate to speak of what they have learned in the confessional, either from the pulpit or in private conversation. This, it was declared, is distasteful to the faithful and is calculated to lesson their confidence.

91 C. 1, X, de cler. non ordinato ministrante, V. 28.

with excommunication *ferendae sententiae* and irregularity as to the reception of higher orders. Urban III decreed[92] that a deacon who would attempt to celebrate Mass should be suspended for a time and should not be promoted to the priesthood. These penalties were confirmed and increased by Gregory XIII,[93] Clement VIII,[94] Urban VIII.[95] Benedict XIV reaffirmed the penalties, declaring that clerics outside the priesthood who would dare to celebrate Mass or hear sacramental confessions should be degraded from their respective orders and committed for punishment to the secular powers.

By the present law the simulation of Holy Mass or the hearing of sacramental confessions, after the manner of a confessor, by one who has not the sacerdotal character is punished with the extreme penalty of excommunication reserved to the Apostolic See in a special manner. The censure, therefore, is not incurred by a priest who, for example, may perform these offices although, by suspension, forbidden to do so. For the present law is intended to prevent intrusion upon the sanctity of these divine offices and to protect the faithful against fraud and deception, and, in the case of Holy Mass, idolatry. Accordingly it would appear that the censure is not incurred by one who would celebrate as a joke or out of derision for the Mass, since the faithful, knowing that the simulator was not a priest and hence could not celebrate, would not be led into the error which the Legislator intends to prevent.

As regards confession, in the present case the simulation of absolution is not necessary for the incurring of the censure. The confession is sacramental so long as the penitent confesses his sins to one whom he assumes to be a priest, even though the one who hears the confession is in reality a lay person and makes no attempt to absolve the penitent.

92 C. 2, X, de cler. non ordin. ministrante, V. 28.

93 Const. *Officii Nostri*, Aug. 6, 1574.

94 Const. *Etsi alias*, Dec. 1, 1601.

95 Const. *Apostolatus Officium*, Mar. 23, 1628.

XVIII. Codex I.C., Can. 2363:

> "Si quis per seipsum vel per alios confessarium de sollicitationis crimine apud Superiores falso denuntiaverit, ipso facto incurrit in excommunicationem speciali modo Sedi Apostolicae reservatam, a quo nequit ullo in casu absolvi, nisi falsam denuntiationem formaliter retractaverit, et damna, si qua inde secuta sint, pro viribus reparaverit, imposita insuper gravi ac diuturna poenitentia, firmo praescripto can. 894."

Although the crime of soliciting a penitent *ad turpia* is indeed heinous, the false accusation of a confessor in so serious a matter is far more grave; for the former may be due to human weakness, but the latter is prompted by hatred, envy or revenge. Thus, Benedict XIV, in the Const. "Sacramentum Penitentiae," June 1, 1741, deplored and condemned the detestable crime of false accusation and reserved the absolution of that sin to the Holy See. Later he extended this reservation to all those who in any manner procured the accusation. And even now this sin is the only one reserved on its own account to the Holy See.[96] However, there is added to the sin, by the law of today, a censure of excommunication, which likewise is reserved to the Holy See, in a special manner.

The accusation, to come under this law, must be that of *sollicitatio ad turpia*, the significance of which is gathered from the Constitution of Benedict XIV, above mentioned, which declares as guilty of this crime priests, secular or religious, who, in the act of sacramental confession or before or immediately after it, or in a confessional or any other place set aside or chosen for confession, solicit or provoke *ad inhonesta et turpia* by words, signs, nods, touches, or writing, any person, or dare to hold with any person unlawful speech or communication.[97]

The accusation must be in itself false and known to be such by the one who makes it. It must be made to the Superior of the Confessor, i.e., made judicially, according

96 Can. 894.

97 Cf. Instr. S. C. S. Off. Feb. 20, 1867: "sive mares sive feminae," par. 1.

to the manner provided by law for the denunciation of the crime of solicitation.[98] Thus, the denunciation must be made directly to the Holy Office or before the Ordinary of the place or his delegate and an ecclesiastical notary, and must be signed and sworn to by the accuser. If the name of the accuser is not given in full, or if the denunciation is made anonymously, the document is devoid of all juridical force, and therefore does not fall under the present censure law.

Here again, it will be noticed, the Legislator has placed certain conditions which are prerequisite to absolution from the censure. The accusation formally made must likewise be formally retracted, in the manner indicated above. The accuser must, as far as in him lies, repair any loss which the confessor has sustained from the false accusation, i.e., he must repair the material losses which may have resulted from suspension from office or benefice, for the spiritual losses which the priest may have suffered cannot be repaired by the delinquent. Finally, the delinquent must perform a grave and long penance, which, by Authors, is held to be such a penance as would be equivalent to some duty which the Church imposes *sub gravi*, as fasting, the hearing of mass, etc., the penance being prolonged for a considerable period which is fixed by some at six months.[99]

98 S. C. S. Off. Feb. 20, 1866, n. 6; July 20, 1890; Acta S. Sedis, XXX, p. 149; Cf. Can. 904.

99 Cf. Ferreres "Theol. Moral." 1919, n. 778, Genicot, "Theol. Moral. Instit." II, n. 347.

In can. 243, 2, we read: "Omnes qui ad Congregationes, Tribunalia, Officia Romanae Curiae pertinent, ad secretum servandum tenentur intra fines et secundum modum ex disciplina unicuique propria determinatum." (Cf. Can. 239, 1, 1.) The natural law demands that those things be sedulously guarded in secrecy which, if divulged, would beget scandal among the faithful or at least redound to the detriment of the reputation of one's neighbor. Accordingly, we find that, by the peculiar discipline of two of the Roman Congregations—the Holy Office and the Consistorial—the censure of excommunication has been attached to the violation of the secrecy which the respective laws impose upon certain persons. These censures are reserved in the strictest manner, being reserved to the Roman Pontiff, even to the exclusion of the "Major Poenitentiarius," except in danger of death. In the S. Congr. of the Holy Office, which, for the most part, must deal with matters of faith, all the "Officials" are bound by oath to maintain secrecy under pain of excommunication. (Cf. Const. *Sapienti Consilio*, June 29, 1908.) This oath of the Holy Office was extended to the Consistorial Congregation, whose Officials also are bound to secrecy under pain of excommunication. Moreover, this obligation extends to all persons who are interrogated in any matter by the Consistorial Congregation. In this connection it will be well to observe a recent response of the Holy Office. The following dubia were presented: I. "Num iis, qui sub secreto S. Officii de informationibus requiruntur circa personas ad episcopatum promovendas liceat delatum sibi munus, qualibet de causa, etiam ad tutiores notitias hauriendas, aliis revelare?" II. "Num, reticita commissione, de qua supra, liceat ab aliis notitias requirere, quoties adsit periculum, etiam remotum, revelationis secreti?" III. "Num datas informationes liceat, quacumque de causa, alteri, etiam secretissimo et intimo, vel in ipsa confessione revelare?" IV. "Quibus poenis plectatur, qui talia egerit in primo vel secundo vel tertio casu?"

Sacra Congregatio, omnibus mature perpensis, ad praedicta dubia respondendum censuit:

Ad I, II, III, In omnibus his casibus non licere.

Ad IV, Excommunicatione, a qua nemo, nisi ipse Romanus Pontifex, excluso etiam Emo. Cardinali Majori Poenitentiario, absolvere potest; aliisque poenis ferendae sententiae quae contra violatores secreti S. Officii a jure statutae sunt. Romae, die 25, April, 1917. Cf. *Acta Ap. Sedis*, 1917, pag. 223.

CHAPTER II

Excommunications Reserved "Simpliciter" to the Apostolic See

The second series of censures contained in the Constitution *Apostolicae Sedis* of Pius IX comprises eighteen sentences of excommunication reserved in a simple manner to the Roman Pontiff. Seven of these, it will be seen, have passed unchanged into the new law; one has been extended as regards the matter concerned; four have suffered more or less diminution in the penalty itself, in its reservation, or in the extent of its application; while six of the excommunications are found to be abrogated.

Here, too, we shall follow the order of the articles of the Constitution of Pius IX.

Const. *Apost. Sedis:*

> "Excommunicationi latae sententiae Romano Pontifici reservatae subjacere declaramus:
>
> "I. Docentes vel defendentes sive publice sive privatim propositiones ab Apostolica Sede damnatas sub excommunicationis poena latae sententiae; item docentes vel defendentes tanquam licitam praxim inquirendi a poenitente nomen complicis, prouti damnata est a Benedicto XIV in Const. 'Suprema' 7 Julii 1745; 'Ubi primum' 2 Julii 1746; 'Ad eradicandum' 28 Septembris 1746."

Codex I.C., Can. 2317:

> "Pertinaciter docentes vel defendentes sive publice sive privatim doctrinam, quae ab Apostolica Sede vel a Concilio Generali damnata quidem fuit, sed non uti formaliter haeretica, arceantur a ministerio praedicandi verbum Dei audiendive sacramentales confessiones et a quolibet docendi munere, salvis aliis poenis quas sententia damnationis forte statuerit, vel quas Ordinarius, post

monitionem, necessarias ad reparandum scandalum duxerit."

Can. 888, 2:

"Caveat omnino (confessarius) ne complicis nomen inquirat . . ."

This article of the Constitution contains two parts, which, in the new law, are treated separately. The former deals with those propositions which have been condemned under pain of excommunication, although they are not formally heretical; for if they contained formal heresy, those teaching or defending them would fall under the censure contained in Art. II of Series I[1] and incur excommunication reserved specially to the Holy See. This distinction is clarified in the new Code, which forbids, by Can. 2317, the teaching or defending of propositions that have been condemned, "but not as formally heretical."

The new law has a wider extension in this case than that of the Constitution. By the latter it was forbidden under penalty to defend or teach not every condemned proposition, but only those condemned under pain of excommunication; the new law comprehends in the present instance every condemned proposition that is not formally heretical,[2] without regard to penalties attached to the condemnation.[3] Again, the Constitution contemplated only those propositions condemned by the Apostolic See, hence not those condemned by a General Council,[4] while the present law includes likewise those condemned by such Councils.[5]

It must be noted here that those penalties, even of excommunication, which the Holy See or a General Council,

1 Can. 2314.

2 Cf. Can. 1325.

3 Cf. Tephany, "Constitution *Apostolicae Sedis*, Tours, 1883, n. 218 ff. Avanzini offers a list of 335 propositions affected by this article of the Constitution, and dating from 1520 to 1752.

4 E. g., those propositions of Wycliffe and Huss condemned in the Council of Constance in 1418.

5 Cf. D'Annibale, l. c., n. 105; Pennachi I, p. 458 ff.

when condemning a proposition, attached to the teaching or defense of such proposition, are still in force and are incurred according to the conditions set down in the particular sentence of condemnation. (The same rule will apply to penalties established in future condemnations.) For Canon 2317, in the clause: "salvis aliis poenis quas sententia damnationis forte statuerit," makes mention, general at least, of such penalties and thus saves them from abrogation, which they would otherwise suffer in virtue of Canon 6, n. 5.

But while the law is now more extensive, the penalty for the violation of it is no longer incurred *ipso facto;* nor is the penalty of excommunication retained, since it is omitted in the Code, which provides that those teaching or defending the condemned propositions be forbidden to preach the Word of God, to hear sacramental confessions or to perform any acts of teaching whatsoever, in addition to which the Ordinary may impose other punishments to repair the scandal resulting from the acts of the delinquents. And, since these penalties are so severe, the new law further requires pertinacity in the delinquent, which implies the disregard of warnings which he shall have received.[6]

The second part of the present article punishes the practice of inquiring of a pentitent in confession the name of his accomplice in sin. The first legislation on this subject is contained in the Encyclical Letter "Suprema," which Pope Benedict XIV, on July 7, 1745, addressed to the bishops of Portugal, where the pernicious practice had become very prevalent on the part of confessors actuated by a false zeal for the correction of sinners. In the following year the same Pontiff found it necessary to repeat his condemnation of these confessors, and in the Const. "Ubi primum," July 2, 1746, imposed the censure of excommunication *latae sententiae,* which he renewed in September of that year[7] and extended to the universal Church and which was confirmed in the Const. *Apost.*

6 Cf. Sole, l. c., n. 324 ff.

7 Const. *Ad eradicandum.*

Sedis by Pius IX. The latter included also the teaching or defending the practice as lawful.

In the new law the traditional disapproval of the practice is confirmed in Can. 888, 2, quoted above, wherein the Legislator treats of the duties of the ministers of Penance. The penalty, called forth, as many others were, by particular needs of the times, is abrogated by omission from the Code,[8] which specifies no punishment in the case.

II. Const. *Apost. Sedis:*

> "Violentas manus, suadente diabolo, iniicientes in clericos, vel utriusque sexus monachos, exceptis quoad reservationem casibus et personis, de quibus jure vel privilegio permittitur ut Episcopus aut alius absolvat."

Codex I.C., Can. 2343, 4:

> "Qui violentas manus . . . injecerit . . . in personam aliorum (scl. quam Rom. Pontificis, S. R. E. Cardinalium, vel Legatorum, vel Patriarchae, Archiepiscopi, Episcopi, etiam titularis) clericorum vel utriusque sexus religiosorum, subjaceat ipso facto excommunicationi Ordinario proprio reservatae, qui praeterea aliis poenis, si res ferat, pro suo prudenti arbitrio eum puniat."

In the preceding chapter[9] we discussed the penalty incurred by those violating the "privilege of the Canon" in so far as it concerns the higher dignitaries of the Church—the Pope, Cardinals, Legates, Patriarchs, Archbishops, and Bishops residential and titular. We also observed that in the new Code the grades of punishment in this matter have been more logically proportioned and better reflect the principle laid down in Can. 2207.

Accordingly, the Const. *Apost. Sedis* now considers those who violate the "privilege of the Canon" in regard to clerics and to Religious of either sex. For these, too, as has been already shown, enjoy this privi-

8 Can. 6, 5.
9 Art. II.

lege.[10] However, as their dignity is less than that of the prelates, the penalty for the violation of their right is less severe, not in nature, since in all cases the penalty is excommunication, but in the degree of reservation of the censure. Thus the excommunication incurred by those who lay violent hands upon clerics or upon Religious of either sex is reserved by law not to the Holy See, as it was formerly, but to the Ordinary of the offender. The Ordinary, under the old law, could absolve only "impuberes," nuns under his jurisdiction, and clerics in seminaries, and these only when the injury inflicted was slight, the crime occult, or recourse to the Holy See difficult. The same power was conceded to prelates who had quasi-episcopal jurisdiction over determinate persons and territory and to Prelates of Regulars for their respective subjects.[11]

The omission by the Legislator of the familiar phrase "Suadente diabolo" [12] implies no limitation of the extent of this law, since these words signify nothing more than gravely sinful action, which, in the Code, is sufficiently provided for in the general law.[13]

III. Const. *Apost. Sedis:*

> "Duellum perpetrantes, aut simpliciter ad illud provocantes, vel ipsum acceptantes, et quoslibet complices, vel qualemcumque operam aut favorem praebentes, necnon de industria spectantes, illudque permittentes, vel quantum in illis est non prohibentes, cujuscumque dignitatis sint, etiam regalis vel imperialis."

Codex I.C., Can. 2351, 1:

> "Servato praescripto Can. 1240, 1, 4, duellum perpetrantes aut simpliciter ad illud provocantes vel ipsum acceptantes vel quamlibet operam aut favorem praebentes, necnon de industria spectantes,

10 C. 8, 17, C. VI, q. 1; C. 9, X, de vita et honestate clericorum, III, 1; C. 29, C. 17, q. 4; Canons 119-123, 488, 1, 614.

11 Conc. Trid. Sess. XXIV, cap. 11, de ref.

12 C. 29, C. 17, q. 4.

13 Can. 2242, 1. Cf. S. Alph. "Theol. Moral." I, 275: "Haec verba non importat scientiam formalem censurae sed tantum peccati."

illudque permittentes vel quantum in ipsis est non prohibentes, cujuscumque dignitatis sint, subsunt ipso facto excommunicationi Sedi Apostolicae simpliciter reservatae."

A duel, in so far as it constitutes an ecclesiastical offense, is a prearranged combat between two or more persons, in equal number on both sides, with deadly weapons involving danger of death, or serious danger of mutilation or wounding.[14] It is contrary to the natural and the Divine positive law. The Church, at an early date, stood out against duelling. Pope Nicholas I (858-867) condemned it (monomachia) as a tempting of God, and the condemnation was reiterated by succeeding popes, among them Alexander III (1159-1181) and Celestine III (1191-1198). Alexander III forbade clerics to enter a duel, under pain of deposition,[15] and Celestine III declared the participants in duels irregular.[16]

From the middle of the fifteenth century duelling for the defense of honor increased, especially in the Romance countries, to so great an extent that the Council of Trent found it necessary to punish duelling with the severest penalties. Thus the Council decreed that "the detestable custom of duelling, which the Devil had originated in order to bring about at the same time the ruin of the soul and the violent death of the body, should be entirely uprooted from the Christian soil." [17] Temporal rulers who permitted duels between Christians in their territories were excommunicated *ipso facto* and lost any jurisdiction which they may have received from the Church. The duellers and their "seconds" and advisors, together with the spectators ("de industria spectantes") were likewise excommunicated and suffered perpetual infamy. Those who were killed in the duel were to be deprived of Christian burial. To this Benedict XIV added that duellists should be denied Chris-

14 Wernz, "Jus Decretalium," n. 375 ss.
15 C. 1, X, de cler. pugn., V, 14.
16 C. 2, X, de cler. pugn., V, 14.
17 Sess. XXV, cap. 19, de ref.

tian burial even if they did not die on the duelling ground and had received absolution before death.[18]

These penalties were confirmed by Pius IX in the Const. *Apost. Sedis,* in the article quoted above, which has been embodied literally in the new Code. (Can. 2351.) However, the former discipline has been relaxed on one point. In the new law it is provided that those who die in a duel, or from a wound received therein, are to be deprived of ecclesiastical burial unless they have given some sign of repentance, which abrogates the contrary legislation of Benedict XIV.

The Code, generally, does not *expressly* mention the accomplices in a specific crime to which a censure is attached. In this respect it differs from the Const. *Apost. Sedis.* Complicity, under the present law, is to be determined by the general rules laid down in Canons 2209 and 2231. Yet, in Can. 2351 several classes of persons, other than the duellers themselves, are expressly named. The reason is that the Legislator considers, and by attaching a penalty declares, that the acts of these persons are distinct crimes, although the censure is not incurred by such persons unless the duel has actually taken place. ("Effectu secuto.")[19]

IV. Const. *Apost. Sedis:*

> "Nomen dantes sectae Massonicae aut Carbonariae, aut aliis ejusdem generis sectis, quae contra Ecclesiam, vel legitimas potestates, seu palam seu clandestine machinantur, necnon iisdem sectis favorem qualemcumque praestantes; earumve occultos corypheos ac duces non denuntiantes donec non denuntiaverint."

Codex I.C., Can. 2335:

> "Nomen dantes sectae Massonicae aliisve ejusdem generis associationibus quae contra Ecclesiam vel legitimas civiles potestates machinantur, contrahunt ipso facto excommunicationem Sedi Apostolicae simpliciter reservatam."

18 Const. *Detestabilem* Nov. 10, 1752; Rituale Romanum, Tit. VI, c. 2, n. 4.

19 Cf. Can. 2209, 7; Capello, l. c., n. 119.

The Masonry here condemned is that systematic method of teaching morality by means of symbols and ritualistic forms according to the principles of modern Freemasonry, which dates from the foundation of the Grand Lodge of England, June 24, 1717. The "Carbonari" comprise the secret political society which sprang up in France and Italy at the beginning of the nineteenth century from the political upheaval consequent upon the French Revolution.

The first papal pronouncement against Freemasons was the Const. "In eminenti," issued by Pope Clement XII,[20] by which he declared all members of the association to be suspected of heresy and to incur *ipso facto* excommunication reserved to the Roman Pontiff. He further directed bishops to apply other due punishments. In this Constitution are indicated the principal reasons why Masonic societies are objectionable from the Catholic, Christian, moral, political and social points of view: (a) the inculcation of religious indifferentism and contempt for orthodoxy and ecclesiastical authority; (b) the inscrutable secrecy and fallacious disguise of the society and its "work"; (c) the oaths of secrecy and fidelity, which cannot bind because the scope is unlawful and wicked; (d) the danger to the tranquillity of the State and to the spiritual health of souls.

Pope Pius VII [21] was the first to condemn the Carbonari, whom he declared "certainly to be an imitation, if not an offshoot, of the Masonic society," for Masons were immediately eligible to the second, or "Master" degree of the Carbonari. Subsequent condemnations were issued by Leo XII,[22] Gregory XVI,[23], Pius IX [24] and Leo XIII.[25] The Congregation of the Inquisition decreed [26]

20 April 28, 1738.
21 Const. *Ecclesiam,* Sept. 13, 1821.
22 Const. *Quo graviora,* Mar. 13, 1825.
23 Enc. litt. *Inter.*
24 Enc. Litt. *Qui pluribus,* Nov. 9, 1846.
25 Enc. Litt. *Humanum Genus,* Apr. 20, 1884.
26 Aug. 5, 1846.

that the secret societies of which the Pontifical Constitutions treated were all those which militate against Church or State, whether or not they exact the oath of secrecy. Accordingly the censure contained in the Const. *Apostolicae Sedis* affected Masons, Carbonari, and the members of all other societies of the same nature. The Carbonari are not mentioned in the new law, since their society has ceased to wield its former influence. Substantially, however, the new law is a confirmation of that of Pius IX, comprehending the same societies and inflicting the same penalties as the law of 1869. However, the provision in the latter, by which the leaders of these condemned societies must, under pain of excommunication, be denounced, is omitted from the law of today. And wisely so, for there are in existence today not a few associations, of divers origin, rites and forms, which are not easily distinguished one from another, so that the obligation to denounce would often be difficult to determine.[27]

V. Const. *Apost. Sedis:*

> "Immunitatem asyli Ecclesiastici ausu temerario violare jubentes aut violantes."

The earliest legislation by the Church on the "right of asylum" is that of Pope St. Leo the Great [28] in 441 A.D., who forbade the betrayal of one who had fled to the Church for refuge. The Councils of Orleans (507), Ilerda (524) and Toledo (681) successively vindicated this immunity of the Church under pain of excommunication.[29] In Germany the rude conception of justice that prevailed in the early days brought about the foundation of this same right, which was subsequently extended to the surroundings of the church, the cemeteries, Bishops' dwellings, monasteries, etc., and was upheld consistently by the various Pontiffs. Since the close of the Middle Ages, however, civil legislation has grown in opposition

27 Cf. Conc. Plen. Balt., III, in append. p. 253. Balto., 1886.

28 C. 6, D. LXXXVII.

29 C. 19, 35, 36, C. XVII, q. 4.

to the ecclesiastical right of asylum, so that the early ecclesiastical laws, by which the lay powers were restricted, have been modified more and more.[30] Thus by the time this natural right is asserted in the Const. *Apost. Sedis* by Pius IX, in which the penalty of excommunication is confirmed for its violation, the clause "ausu temerario" is inserted in the law, which reduces its extent to a minimum, since it would rarely happen that the law would be violated by anyone not impelled by civil duties.

The censure is therefore rendered useless in practice and for this reason is omitted from the law now prevailing. As a legitimate principle, however, the right of asylum is reasserted and is given expression in the Code in these terms: "Ecclesia jure asyli gaudet ita ut rei. qui ad illam confugerint, inde non sunt extrahendi, nisi necessitas urgeat, sine assensu Ordinarii vel saltem rectoris ecclesiae." [31]

VI. Const. *Apost. Sedis:*

> "Violantes clausuram monialium cujuscumque generis aut conditionis, sexus vel aetatis fuerint, in earum monasteria absque legitima licentia ingrediendo; pariterque eos introducentes, vel admittentes, itemque moniales ab illa exeuntes extra casus ac formam a S. Pio V in Const. "Decori" praescriptam."

Codex I.C., Can. 2342:

> "Plectuntur ipso facto excommunicatione Sedi Apostolicae simpliciter reservata: 1. Clausuram monialium violantes cujuscumque generis aut conditionis vel sexus sint, in earum monasteria sine legitima licentia ingrediendo, pariterque eos introducentes vel admittentes . . . 3. Moniales e clausura illegitime exeuntes contra praescriptum Can. 601."

Although the female religious were not bound by the law of the cloister until the time of Boniface VIII, yet

30 Cf. Greg. XIV, Const. *Cum alias*, May 24, 1591; Bened. XIII, Const. *Ex quo*, June 8, 1725; Clem. XII, Const. *Supremo justitiae*, Jan. 1, 1734; Bened. XIV, Const. *Officii Nostri*, Mar. 15, 1750.

31 Can. 1179.

it has always been the mind of the Church that they live apart from the world. This is clearly manifest from Councils so early as those of Carthage (397) and Orleans (552). The cloister, however, was not universally kept and the discipline of the various bishops was not uniform, which gave rise to scandals and contentions. Boniface VIII in the celebrated Const. "Periculoso" decreed that all nuns, whether expressly or tacitly professed, must remain within the cloister perpetually,[32] unless they had legitimate cause for leaving, together with the permission of the Superior. Disregard for this law resulted in the more severe restrictions of the Council of Trent, which renewed the aforesaid Constitution and forbade, under pain of excommunication *latae sententiae,* any nun to leave, even for a short time, without the permission of the Bishop; or any other person to enter a cloister without the Bishop's permission in writing.[33]

Pius V confirmed the Tridentine law and determined the various causes for which one might lawfully leave the cloister.[34] In 1575 Gregory XIII recalled all faculties by which laics might enter the cloisters of women,[35] and declared excommunication *latae sententiae* and reserved to the Roman Pontiff to be incurred by those who admitted such persons.

Pius IX in the Const. *Apost. Sedis* merely renewed the previous discipline, inflicting the censure upon those entering the cloister of nuns without permission, those admitting them, and nuns who leave the cloister without sufficient cause approved by the Ordinary. This rule, slightly changed, still obtains.[36]

The law of 1869 forbade the entrance of any person, no matter what his or her age. The Code does not retain

32 C. un. de Statu Relig. III, 16, in Sexto.

33 Sess. XXV, cap. 5, de reg.

34 Const. *Decori,* Feb. 1, 1570.

35 Const. *Ubi Gratia.*

36 Can. 597. In conformity with the decree of the S. Congr. de Relig., dated Nov. 7, 1916, postulants are, during the period of their postulancy, required to observe the law of the cloister. However, this does not render them liable to the present censure, which affects only those who have made solemn profession.

the expression "*cujuscumque aetatis,*" because this would contradict the general law which excuses "impuberes" from all punishments *latae sententiae.* (Can. 2230.) The former law embraced also those who had not reached the age of puberty (which, in penal law, was considered to be the completion of the fourteenth year), unless they were under seven years of age, or infants.[37] Today the age of puberty in all cases is fourteen years for males and twelve for females; and only after these respective ages have been attained can a *latae sententiae* penalty be incurred.

VII. Const. *Apost. Sedis:*

> "Mulieres violantes regularium virorum clausuram, et superiores aliosve eas admittentes."

Codex I.C., Can. 2342:

> "Plectuntur ipso facto excommunicatione Sedi Apostolicae simpliciter reservata: . . . 2. Mulieres violantes regularium virorum clausuram et superiores aliique, quicumque ii sint, eas cujuscumque aetatis introducentes vel admittentes."

With regard to the violation of the cloister of male religious the former law has undergone little change. Only women are forbidden to enter this cloister, whereas neither men nor women may enter the cloister of nuns. Those under the age of twelve years, while they are also forbidden to enter the cloister of men, do not incur the censure, in virtue of Can. 2230, as explained in the preceding article.

Formerly it was held [38] that the censure was not incurred by persons outside the monastery who permitted women to enter. It was argued that only one living inside a place could be said to grant entrance to that place, and that consequently no one outside the monastery was comprehended by the law. However just this benign interpretation may have been, the new law expressly for-

37 Cf. Wernz, VI, n. 78; Schmalzgrueber, L. V., Tit. 23, n. 4 ss; D'Annibale, l. c., n. 123.

38 Cf. D'Annibale, l. c., n. 128.

bids not only the admission, but also the "introduction" of women, for by this the law of the cloister is likewise violated.[39]

It is further specified in the new law that females of any age whatsoever are excluded, which obviates the interpretation formerly advanced, that the admission of girls under seven years of age did not merit the excommunication.[40]

It is seen, then, that from the cloister of men the law excludes, under pain of the censure, women only, and indeed all of these, except the wives of kings, presidents, or other actual rulers of the State (Can. 598, 2), while both men and women of any age or station are forbidden to enter the cloister of nuns. Moreover, it is only nuns, properly so-called (Can. 488, 7), who are forbidden under pain of excommunication to leave their respective cloisters without due permission.

VIII. Const. *Apost. Sedis:*

> "Reos simoniae realis in beneficiis quibuscumque, eorumque complices."

IX.

> "Reos simoniae confidentialis in beneficiis quibuslibet cujuscunque sint dignitatis."

X.

> "Reos simoniae realis ob ingressum in religionem."

Codex I.C., Can. 2392:

> "Firmo praescripto Can. 729, delictum perpetrantes simoniae in quibuslibet officiis, beneficiis aut dignitatibus ecclesiasticis: 1. Incurrunt in excommunicationem latae sententiae Sedi Apostolicae simpliciter reservatam; . . . "

Simony, so named from Simon Magus,[41] may be of divine or of ecclesiastical law. The former is defined as

39 Cf. Chap. V, Art. II.
40 Cf. Pennachi, I, p. 789.
41 Acts VIII, 18-24.

"the deliberate intention of buying or selling for a temporal price a thing intrinsically spiritual, or annexed unto spiritual things in such a way that the temporal thing cannot exist without the spiritual, or the spiritual thing is the object, partial at least, of a contract." The trading of spiritual things in kind, or of temporal things annexed to spiritual, or even of purely temporal things when this is forbidden by the Church to prevent irreverence to spiritual things, constitutes simony of the ecclesiastical law. (Can. 727.)

The crime of simony was formally condemned as early as the fifth century, when Pope Leo the Great declared that simoniacal bishops, priests and deacons and all who communicated with them should be excommunicated.[42] The present articles of the Constitution are also of long standing. The censure for simony in the matter of entrance into religion dates back to the year 1262, in the pontificate of Urban IV.[43] Paul II, in 1464, excommunicated all guilty of real simony in ecclesiastical benefices, together with their accomplices;[44] while Pius IV introduced the same punishment for confidential simony,[45] which was confirmed by Pius V.[46]

The new law makes no distinction in the matter of punishment between *"real"* and *"confidential"* simony.[47] Nor does it mention specifically simony in connection with entrance into religion, because the definition of simony given in Can. 727 comprehends all these species.

Benefices alone were mentioned in Articles VIII and IX of the Constitution of Pius IX. From this it was justly concluded that unless the simony was perpetrated in regard to benefices strictly so-called the censure was

42 Council of Chalcedon, 451.

43 C. 1, de simonia, V. 1, in Extrav. Comm.

44 C. 2, de Simonia V. 1, in Extrav. Comm.

45 Const. *Romanum Pontificem*, Oct. 17, 1564.

46 Const. *Intolerabilis*, June 1, 1569.

47 "Real," when the stipulations of mutual agreement have been either partly or completely carried out by both parties; "Confidential," when a benefice is procured for a certain person with the understanding that he will either resign it in favor of the one through whom he obtained it or divide with him the revenues.

not incurred.[48] There are, however, many other ecclesiastical things which may become the object of simoniacal practice, as chaplaincies, temporary vicariates, pensions and dignities of divers kinds. Wisely, then, the law has been extended so as to embrace every office, benefice and dignity in the Church. Because we are here dealing *in odiosis*, it seems that "office" should be taken in a strict sense and hence restricted to those which have been permanently established by divine or ecclesiastical law, are conferred according to the regulations laid down in Canon Law, and carry with them some participation of ecclesiastical power, whether of Orders or of jurisdiction. (Canon 145.)

XI. Const. *Apost. Sedis:*

> "Omnes quaestum facientes ex indulgentiis aliisque gratiis spiritualibus, excommunicationis censura plectuntur Constitutione S. Pii V 'Quam plenum' 2 Jan., 1569."

Codex I.C., Can. 2327:

> "Quaestum facientes ex indulgentiis plectuntur ipso facto excommunicatione Sedi Apostolicae simpliciter reservata."

In the Middle Ages, when funds were needed to support some worthy object, alms were solicited of the faithful. Thus, for example, the early crusades were made possible. The almsgiving and other pious works gained for the donors certain stipulated indulgences. To systematize the publication of these indulgences and the collection of the alms the bishops entrusted these matters to "Quaestores," or "Praedicatores quaestuosi," as they were called. These were not all worthy of their trust. Many of them were self-seekers and even preached false doctrine in their quest for gain.

Clement V in the Council of Vienne (1311) sharply rebuked the "Quaestores" and ordered them to be punished. The abuses, nevertheless, increased and gave rise to many other evils, and in the sixteenth century afforded the occasion for the far-reaching heresy of Martin Luther. The Council of Trent decreed that the name and methods of the "Quaestores" be forever abolished, and committed the publication of indulgences and the receiving of alms to Local Ordinaries, without remuneration.[49] Nevertheless, under the pretext of special privileges, certain "Quaestores" continued the illicit practice of preaching and collecting. Wherefore Pius V formally cancelled all indulgences the gaining of which was conditioned by alms-giving.[50] He also imposed, in 1569, excommunication *latae sententiae* reserved to the Roman Pontiff upon all, bishops excepted, who thenceforth engaged in any traffic in indulgences or other spiritual favors,[51] which censure was confirmed by Pius IX as quoted above.

By the law of today the same censure is incurred for traffic in indulgences, but no mention is made of "other spiritual favors." These were thus exclusively enumerated in the Const. "Quam plenum": the faculty of choosing a confessor to absolve one from sins or censures; the celebration of Mass and Ecclesiastical burial during the time of interdict; the use of forbidden foods; the use of two or more sponsors in Baptism;[52] and absolution from the censure resulting from real simony and reserved to the Roman Pontiff.

The Const. "Quam plenum" did not bind bishops or higher dignitaries under pain of excommunication, but rather of interdict *ab ingressu ecclesiae* and loss of the fruits of their benefices. Under the present discipline (Can. 2392) bishops cannot be exempted since the law makes no exception in their favor,[53] while Cardinals, since they are not expressly included, are by law exempt.

48 Cf. D'Annibale, n. 128.

49 Sess. XXI, cap. 9, de ref; cf. Pennachi I, 928.

50 Const. *Etsi Dominici*, Feb. 8, 1567.

51 Const. *Quam plenum*, Jan. 2, 1569.

52 Conc. Trid. Sess. XXIV, cap. 2, de ref. matr.

53 Cf. Can. 2237, 2.

XII. Const. *Apost. Sedis:*

> "Colligentes eleemosynas majoris pretii pro Missis, et ex iis lucrum captantes, faciendo eas celebrari in locis ubi Missarum stipendia minoris pretii esse solent."

Codex I.C., Can. 2324:

> "Qui deliquerint contra praescriptum Can. 827, 828, 840, 1, ab Ordinario pro gravitate culpae puniantur, non exclusa, si res ferat, suspensione aut beneficii vel officii ecclesiastici privatione, vel, si de laicis agatur, excommunicatione."

The present censure was derived by Pius IX from the Const. of Benedict XIV "Quanta cura," dated June 30, 1741 in which he forbade traffic in Mass stipends under pain of excommunication for laymen and suspension for clerics. Pius IX, however, extended the censure of excommunication to all persons guilty of the crime.

This penalty has been abrogated by the Code of 1918, although the Church by no means ceases to denounce the nefarious dealing. She expressly forbids the semblance of negotiation and trading in Mass stipends.[54] She requires that every contract by which a stipend, however small, is accepted, whether for the celebration or for the application of Mass, must be satisfied.[55] And when "manual" [56] stipends are transferred by the priest who has received them to another priest the entire amount of the stipend must be given over, unless the donor expressly permits that a part of the stipend be retained, or the amount in excess of the customary stipend was certainly intended for the priest to whom the stipend was first given. These are some of the many regulations which the new law contains on the subject.[57]

However, the penalty for contravening these laws is

54 Can. 827: "A stipe Missarum etiam species negotiationis vel mercaturae omnino arceatur."

55 Can. 828.

56 Stipends offered "off-hand," as it were, by the faithful for Masses, out of pure devotion, or by reason of an obligation imposed by a testator upon his heirs.

57 Cf. Codex I. C., Lib. III, Tit. II, Art. IV.

no longer incurred *ipso facto.* The Ordinary, considering the individual delinquencies, will punish infractions of the laws just mentioned (Can. 827, 828, 840, 1) with the means that he deems most suitable. Clerics may be suspended or deprived of their benefices or offices if their cases warrant this; but the censure of excommunication is to be inflicted only upon laymen who engage in the unlawful traffic, since they seldom have occasion to deal with the transfer of Mass stipends and their participation in the illicit dealing is especially odious.[58]

The manual Mass stipend is fixed by the Local Ordinary, or, in lieu of his decree, by the diocesan custom. In excess of this amount nothing can be demanded by any priest, secular or religious. (Can. 831.)

XIII. Const. *Apost. Sedis:*

> "Omnes qui excommunicatione multantur in Constitutionibus S. Pii V. 'Admonet Nos,' 4 Kalendas Aprilis, 1567, Innocent IX 'Quae ab hac Sede,' pridie Nonas Novembris, 1591, Clementis VIII 'Ad Romani Pontificis Curam,' 29 Jun., 1592, et Alexandri VII 'Inter ceteras' nono Kalendas Novembris 1660, alienationem et infeudationem civitatum et locorum S.R.E. respicientibus."

In the sixteenth century it was found that many abuses had resulted from the enfoeffment of lands belonging to the Roman Church. While retaining the dominion over all properties, several earlier Pontiffs had seen fit to grant to private persons the use and administration of certain sections of the Papal territory, and now the Holy See was besieged with requests for further grants, by Cardinals, temporal princes and other high personages. It was to put an end to this practice, so fraught with abuses, that Pius V published the Const. "Admonet Nos",[59] in which he declared excommunication reserved to the Roman Pontiff to be incurred *ipso facto* by any person whatsoever who attempted to persuade

58 Cf. Chap. III, Art. IV.
59 May 23, 1567.

the Roman Pontiff to alienate (reserving the dominion) cities, towns, camps, places, etc., belonging to the Roman Church. It mattered not whether the requests were prompted by avarice or by zeal for the apparent utility of the Church, or for what length of time the grant was to last.[60] With slight changes the law of Pius V was renewed and confirmed by succeeding Pontiffs: Gregory XIII,[61] Sixtus V,[62], Gregory XIV,[63] Innocent IX,[64] Clement VIII,[65] and Alexander VII.[66]

Pius IX, in the Const. *Apost. Sedis,* simply reaffirmed the censure that had been in force since the time of Pius V. He retained it as a means of safeguarding the integrity of the temporal dominions of the Holy See during the deplorable years that marked his pontificate. The censure has been omitted from the new law since conditions in Italy at the present time do not admit of the practice which this censure was intended to combat. For this law did not comprehend alienation properly so-called, by which all right to property is transferred, but rather enfoeffment, whereby the Church retained the "jus in rem."

XIV. Const. *Apost. Sedis:*

> "Religiosos praesumentes clericis aut laicis extra casum necessitatis sacramentum Extremae Unctionis aut Eucharistiae per Viaticum ministrare absque parochi licentia."

Not a few of the censures contained in the Const. *Apos. Sedis* took their rise from temporarily prevalent abuses and ceased to be required when their purpose had been fulfilled and the abuses abolished. The present article contains such a censure. During the pontificate of

60 Cit. Const.
61 *Inter cetera,* May 27, 1572.
62 *Quanta Apostolicae,* Mar. 18, 1586.
63 *Romanus Pontifex,* Dec. 19, 1590.
64 *Quae ab hac,* Nov. 4, 1591.
65 *Ad Romani,* Feb. 14, 1592.
66 *Inter ceteras,* Oct. 24, 1660.

Clement V (1305-1314) complaints were brought to that Pontiff that the rights of parish priests were being invaded by Religious. These latter had, in the course of many years, accumulated extensive privileges from the Roman Pontiffs. Actuated by zeal for souls, many Religious did not hesitate to infringe upon the rights of parochial clergy in the administration of the Sacraments.[67] Wherefore Pope Clement, in the Council of Vienne (1312), forbade Religious, under pain of excommunicatione *latae sententiae* and reserved to the Roman Pontiff, to administer the Sacraments of Extreme Unction and Holy Eucharist as Viaticum to clerics or laymen, or to solemnize marriage, without having obtained the special permission of the parish priest.[68] Pius IX, renewing the censure in 1869, confined the law to Holy Viaticum and Extreme Unction, so that thenceforth a Religious who solemnized marriage without the permission of the pastor would no longer incur the censure, although he would be guilty of grave sin. Moreover, a special permission was not required by Pius IX, so that even the presumed permission would justify the ministration of the Religious.

The need of a penalty in this matter being no longer urgent, the present censure, like many others, has been omitted from the newly promulgated law. With certain limitations, the rights of pastors to administer the Sacrament of Extreme Unction and to bring Holy Viaticum, publicly or privately, to the sick are clearly set forth in the Code,[69] but to dwell upon these does not fall within the scope of the present work.

XV. Const. *Apost. Sedis:*

> "Extrahentes absque legitima venia reliquias ex sacris coemeteriis, sive catacumbis Urbis Romae, ejusque territorii, eisque auxilium vel favorem praebentes."

67 Penn. I, p. 104.

68 C. 1, de privilegiis et excessibus, V, 7, in Clem.

69 Can. 850, 938, 2, 462.

The systematic exploration of Subterranean Rome dates from the end of the sixteenth century, when Antonio Bosio (1576-1629) undertook the extensive research recorded in his "Roma Sotteranea." The discovery of the many remains of the holy Martyrs and Confessors naturally inspired the faithful with the desire to possess these historic relics and led to indiscriminate searching for the remains of the early Christians. However, not all who were buried in the catacombs were Martyrs or Confessors, and hence there was danger of mistaking false relics for true ones and of exposing to the faithful objects unworthy of veneration.

Paul V, therefore,[70] forbade the removal of the sacred remains under pain of excommunication reserved to the Roman Pontiff,[71] which decree he renewed in the following year,[72] extending the censure to rectors of churches, cemeteries and pious places, who permitted the removal of relics. Notwithstanding these severe penalties men continued to remove the remains from the catacombs and to distribute them widely and indiscriminately, thus causing great scandal to the faithful and often bringing ridicule upon our holy religion. Clement X thereupon published the Const. *Ex commissae Nobis*,[73] in which he confirmed the censure enacted by Paul V and established rules for the worship, conservation and exposition of the holy relics.[74]

The law, as recast by Pius IX, embraced only those who carried away the sacred remains and those who cooperated with them. He retained the law not so much to prevent indiscriminate exploration as to safeguard the faithful from occasions of false veneration. And, since all excavations in the catacombs and cemeteries of Rome are now supervised by the "Commission of Sacred Archeology," founded in 1851 by Pius IX, the danger of pro-

70 Aug. 24, 1613.

71 Cf. Bonacina, "De Excommun." Disp. II, Qu. III, p. XIII.

72 May 16, 1614.

73 Jan. 13, 1672.

74 Cf. Pennachi, 1031 ss.

fanation and deception in regard to the sacred relics is reduced to a minimum. Again, this law had reference to a particular place and hence did not directly affect the Universal Church. In view of these facts it is not surprising that no mention of the censure or of the prohibition is found in the new Code.

XVI. Const. *Apost. Sedis:*

> Communicantes cum excommunicato nominatim a Papa in crimine criminoso, ei scilicet impendendo auxilium et favorem."

Codex I.C., Can. 2338, 2:

> "Impendentes quodvis auxilium vel favorem excommunicato vitando in delicto propter quod excommunicatus fuit . . . ipso facto incurrunt in excommunicationem Sedi Apostolicae simpliciter reservatam."

The communication which is here condemned and punished consists in lending to the excommunicated person any aid or favor in the very offense which merited the excommunication, thereby retarding the repentance of the delinquent. The peculiar malice of this communication lies in the contempt of the supreme authority by which the censure was inflicted and in lessening the efficacy of the medicinal punishment.[75]

The censure was first imposed by Pope Innocent III, May 14, 1199. Thenceforth excommunication reserved to the Roman Pontiff was incurred by anyone who knowingly communicated *in crimine criminoso* with a person excommunicated *nominatim,* either by the Pope or a bishop.[76] Martin V mitigated this law, making the distinction between the "vitandi" and the "tolerati" and holding only those persons to be "vitandi" who had been *nominatim* excommunicated, or whose excommunication was caused by a notorious crime of laying violent

75 Cf. Wernz, VI, n. 360; D'Annibale, l. c., n. 159; Pennachi, l. c., 1041.

76 C. 29, X, de sent. V, 39.

hands upon clerics.[77] Pius IX, in confirming the law, excluded crass and supine ignorance as an excuse for exemption from the censure, but confined the law to those who were excommunicated *nominatim* by the Pope.

The extent of the law is again curtailed with the promulgation of the new Code, inasmuch as the class of "excommunicati vitandi" has been further restricted. Henceforth no one is *vitandus* unless he has been excommunicated *nominatim* by the Apostolic See, the censure pubicly proclaimed (e. g., published in the *Acta Apost. Sedis*) and the stipulation made in the Apostolic decree or sentence that he must be avoided.[78]

It may be noted here that the Const. *Apost. Sedis* forbade communication with one "excommunicated by the Pope, etc.," whereas Can. 2258, 2 reads "excommunicated by the Apostolic See." According to Canon 7, "Apostolic See" includes the Roman Congregations, unless the contrary is evident from the nature of the case or from the context. In the present case there seems to be an extension of the law,[79] since there appears to be no reason why the extent of the term should be restricted to the Pope, although the entire history of this censure has been one of limitation, not, indeed, in favor of the person censured, but of the faithful, with respect to whom the person is "vitandus." [80]

XVII. Const. *Apost. Sedis:*

> "Clerici scienter et sponte communicantes in divinis cum personis a Romano Pontifice nominatim excommunicatis, et ipsos in officiis recipientes."

Codex I.C., Can. 2338, 2:

> " . . . Clerici scienter et sponte in divinis cum eodem (excommunicato vitando) communicantes et ipsum in divinis officiis recipientes ipso facto incurrunt in excommunicationem Sedi Apostolicae simpliciter reservatam."

77 Const. *Ad evitanda* in the Council of Constance, 1418.

78 Can. 2258, 2.

79 Cf. Chelodi, "Jus Poenale," Tridenti, 1920, n. 36.

80 Cf. Const. *Ad evitanda.*

Besides communication "in crimine criminoso" there is another species of communication which the Const. *Apost. Sedis* punished with like censure, namely, communication *in divinis* with and receiving into divine offices clerics whom the Roman Pontiff has excommunicated *nominatim.* This censure also is of long standing, having been instituted by Pope Clement III (1187-1191).[81] It has remained unchanged since it was first enacted and appears in the new Code in its original form. There is, therefore, little to be said upon it in this work.

The "communication" and the "reception" are to be taken conjunctively, this being the more favorable interpretation and more generally adopted by canonists.[82] By Divine Offices are meant the functions of the power of Orders, which have been instituted by Christ or His Church for divine worship and which clerics only can perform. (Can. 2256, 1.) Wherefore clerics only are liable to the censure.[83] However, from these functions we must exclude that of preaching the Divine Word, for this obviously is not comprehended under the present law since, according to Can. 2259, 1, no excommunicated person is deprived by his censure of the right to assist at this service.

Since the Code prohibits communication and reception of *vitandi* as such, we must here also take cognizance of the limitation which the Legislator has placed upon the class of *vitandi*, in Can. 2258, 2, and which was discussed in the preceding article, for in so far as this class is restricted the present censure's extension is curtailed.

Finally, it has been mooted among authors whether "clerici" here includes on the one hand bishops, and on the other Religious who have received the first tonsure. Pennachi, commenting upon the measure, held that both were exempt, the bishops, because they were never desig-

81 C. 18, X, de sent. excomm. V, 39.

82 Suarez, "De Censuris" Disp. X, Sect. II, n. 3; Bonacina, "De excomm. in part." Disp. II, Qu. V, p. III, n. 3; Pennachi, l. c., 1057 ss; D'Annibale, l. c., n. 152.

83 Cf. Can. 108, 1.

nated under the class of "clerics" and because this law is not stated in general terms, as "quilibet," "quicumque," etc.; the Religious, because it is a penal law and should be restricted and because the law usually distinguishes between clerics and religious, as when it censures those who lay violent hands upon "clericos vel monachos utriusque sexus." He also cites Schmalzgrueber,[84] Reiffenstuel,[85] and others. This interpretation seems hardly tenable today in the light of the new Code. For if the Legislator wished to distinguish between clerics and religious in penal matters he would have done so, it may be presumed. Yet no distinction has been made. All who have received the first tonsure are clerics (Can. 108, 1.), whether they be seculars or religious, and hence there is no reason why religious, if they have received the tonsure, should not be included under Can. 2338, 2.[86] As to bishops, we have already had occasion to observe[87] that these must be expressly mentioned in the law in order that they may incur *latae sententiae* punishments of suspension or interdict,[88] a concession granted lest they be prevented too easily from discharging the duties of their office. But exemption from the censure of excommunication is not included in this concession. Moreover, the purpose of the present censure is to safeguard the supreme authority of the Pope, which may, hypothetically, be impugned by bishops as well as by clerics of lesser rank. It seems, therefore, that under the present law bishops also are liable to the excommunication.

XVIII. Const. *Apost. Sedis:*

> "Absolvere praesumentes, etiam quovis praetextu, ab excommunicationibus Romano Pontificii reservatis speciali modo, dummodo non agatur de mortis articulo, in quo tamen firma sit quoad absolutos obligatio standi mandatis Ecclesiae, si convaluerint."

84 Lib. V, T. 39, n. 336.
85 Lib. V, T. 39, n. 187.
86 Cf. D'Annibale, l. c., n. 152, note 11.
87 Chap. I, Art. VIII.
88 Can. 2227, 2.

Codex I.C., Can. 2338, 1:

> "Absolvere praesumentes sine debita facultate, ab excommunicatione latae sententiae specialissimo vel speciali modo Sedi Apostolicae reservata, incurrunt ipso facto in excommunicationem Sedi Apostolicae simpliciter reservatam."

Reservation, in the present sense, is an act by which a superior excludes the absolution of a censure or censures from the power of jurisdiction which he concedes to inferiors. The right of the Supreme Pontiff to restrict jurisdiction follows from the Divine Constitution of the Church. Hence the Council of Trent says: "Merito Pontifices Maximi, pro suprema potestate sibi in Ecclesia universa tradita, causas aliquas criminum graviores suo potuerunt peculiari judicio reservare."[89] Those who impugned this right have met with the condemnation of the Church. Thus, Pope Clement V, in the Council of Vienne (1312), punished those Religious who absolved from censures reserved to the Roman Pontiff or to Local Ordinaries.[90] Sixtus IV in 1748 declared excommunication to be incurred *ipso facto* by those who, except in danger of death, absolved from the censures reserved in a special manner to the Holy See, and contained in the Bull *In Coena Domini*.[91]

This is the censure which Pius retained in his revision of Censures in 1869. It is likewise retained in the new Code, as cited above. The law is restricted today, as it was by the Constitution, to censures *latae sententiae* reserved in a special manner to the Holy See. But, since some censures are now formally reserved *specialissimo modo* to the Holy See, these censures are also included in the newly promulgated law.[92]

The Constitution of 1869 excepted one case in which absolution from specially reserved censures might be given and the present censure not incurred, namely, in danger of death, in which case the penitent, if he recov-

89 Sess. XIV, cap. 7, de poenit.

90 C. 1, de Privilegiis, V, 7, in Clem.

91 C. 5, de Poenitent., V, 9, in Extravag. Comm.

92 See Chap. I, Art. V, X and XIV.

ered from his illness, was obliged, under pain of falling again under the censure, to have recourse, personally or through the confessor, to the Holy See, or at least to seek absolution from one endowed with faculties for absolving from such censures.[93]

The Holy Office later decreed[94] that, in more urgent cases when to defer absolution would cause grave scandal or infamy, the confessor could absolve directly from the censure specially reserved, but must require the penitent, under pain of again incurring the censure, to have the recourse mentioned above. And it was further declared that, even if there were no danger of scandal or infamy, but it would be a hardship for the penitent to remain in mortal sin until the requirements of the law could be observed—even then, any confessor might absolve directly from the censure, the obligation of recourse remaining.[95] The Sacred Penitentiary decided that the penitent need not have recourse through the very confessor who has absolved him, but may do so through any other confessor or even personally, when he has a reasonable cause.[96] In fact, the Holy Office excused the penitent entirely from the obligation of recourse when the recourse is morally impossible, as when neither the penitent nor the confessor is able to send the required letter and no other confessor can be reached.[97]

All these concessions have been embodied in the newly promulgated law, under Can. 2254, and constitute the faculties by which censures reserved *speciali* or *specialissimo modo* to the Apostolic See can be absolved by simple confessors. Ordinarily the confessor or other person absolving must have special power in order to absolve from censures reserved *speciali modo* to the Apostolic See and very special power when the censure is reserved *specialissimo modo*.[98]

93 Cf. Conc. Trid., Sess. XIV, cap. 7, de Poenit.
94 June 30, 1886.
95 S. Off., June 16, 1897.
96 May 22, 1888.
97 Nov. 9, 1898.
98 Can. 2253, 3; Cf. Can. 2237, 3.

XIX. We find in the new Code one new censure of excommunication reserved *simpliciter* to the Apostolic See. Thus:

Codex I.C., Can. 2405:

> "Vicarius Capitularis aliive omnes tam de Capitulo, quam extranei, qui documentum quodlibet ad Curiam episcopalem pertinens sive per se sive per alium subtraxerint vel destruxerint vel celaverint vel substantialiter immutaverint, incurrunt ipso facto in excommunicationem Sedi Apostolicae simpliciter reservatam."

It will be readily seen that the archives of any diocese contain documents of importance to the interests of the Church and of individuals. Records affecting state of life; rights of persons, physical and moral; records of contentious, criminal and penal proceedings, of properties, and of many very personal and important matters which demand the utmost secrecy or may be required for the sake of truth and justice; these are all to be found in the average diocesan archives. It is not surprising, then, that the Church lays stress upon the importance of guarding well the privacy and security of important documents, especially in the event of a See vacated or prevented from functioning. (Can. 374-384.) The present new censure is restricted to such an event, it would appear from the mention of the Vicar Capitular, who does not exist in other cases.[99] So important does the Church regard this security that she now threatens with excommunication reserved to the Holy See any one who steals, destroys, conceals or substantially changes a document belonging to the episcopal Curia.

The censure is specifically inflicted upon the Vicar Capitular and the Cathedral Chapter (Administrator and Diocesan Consultors in the United States, Can. 423), and in general upon any other person, lay or cleric, whether connected with the diocesan Curia or not. It

99 Cf. Cerato, "Censurae Vigentes," n. 88; Cavigioli, "De Censuris Latae Sententiae," n. 153.

matters not, for the law does not distinguish, whether the document be of a public or a private nature, nor whom or what it concerns, so long as it belongs to the Curia. However, it seems proper to exclude documents lent or committed to the Curia by others whose property they are.[100]

To incur the censure by changing a document it is necessary that the substance of it be affected, so that the sense principally intended by the author is altered, or the force of proof which the document certainly had is rendered uncertain or doubtful. The other species of act reprobated in the law require no explanation.

Finally, the censure is incurred not only by those who personally take, destroy, conceal or change a document, but those also in whose name the forbidden acts are performed. Co-operators, of course, if their participation in the offense is such that without it the offense would not have been committed, are likewise guilty and fall under the censure of excommunication.

100 Cf. Chelodi, "Jus Poenale," n. 109; Cavigioli, l. c.; Cerato, l. c., takes the opposite view.

CHAPTER III

EXCOMMUNICATIONS LATAE SENTENTIAE RESERVED TO THE ORDINARY

The Third Series in the Constitution *Apostolicae Sedis* contained three censures of excommunication *latae sententiae* reserved not to the Roman Pontiff, but to Bishops, or Ordinaries. In the present chapter these will be discussed in the light of the new Code. In addition to these, seven censures of excommunication, similarly reserved, will claim attention here, one of which was enacted by Pope Leo XIII in the Const. *Vigilanti studio,* dated May 25, 1893, the others being found for the first time in the Code itself.[1]

Const. *Apost. Sedis:* "Excommunicationi latae sententiae Episcopis sive Ordinariis reservatae subjacere declaramus:

> I. "Clericos in sacris constitutos vel Regulares aut Moniales post votum sollemne castitatis matrimonium contrahere praesumentes; necnon omnes cum aliqua ex praedictis personis matrimonium contrahere praesumentes."

Codex I.C., Can. 2388, 1:

> "Clerici in sacris constituti vel regulares aut moniales post votum sollemne castitatis, itemque omnes cum aliqua ex praedicitis personis matrimonium etiam civiliter tantum contrahere praesumentes, incurrunt in excommunicationem latae sententiae Sedi Apostolicae simpliciter reservatam; . . . "

Clerics in Sacred Orders and Religious have, from the earliest centuries, been forbidden to enter the married

1 Cann. 2319, 2326, 2385 and 2388.

state.[2] The former were forbidden to marry under pain of such penalties as suspension, privation of benefice and deposition. Monks and Consecrated Virgins who contracted marriage were obliged to do severe public penances, and, if they remained contumacious, were perpetually excommunicated.[3] However, it is not until the fourteenth century that we find the violation of this law punished with excommunication *latae sententiae.* Pope Clement V, in the Council of Vienne,[4] enacted the censure which, with certain modifications, has been in force up to the present time. The penalty was incurred *ipso facto* by all who contracted marriage with nuns (*moniales*), and also by regulars, nuns and clerics in Sacred Orders who contracted marriage at all.

Confirmed by Pius IX in the Constitution above quoted, this censure has been in force up to the present day. However, Pius IX did not renew the law as it stood, but made certain extensions and limitations of its scope. Thus, the Clementine law comprehended all religious, without distinction, while that of Pius IX was limited to religious, regulars or nuns, who had been solemnly professed; the former embraced all those who contracted marriage with nuns, hence no women were included on this score, while by the law of 1869 all the necessary accomplices, i. e., the contracting parties, whether men or women, were liable to the censure; finally, the censure of Clement V was not reserved, while that of Pius IX was reserved to the Ordinary, even though the parties to the unlawful marriage had separated. The original censure, then, was considerably modified in 1869.

As the law comes to us in the Code one important change is made, not in the nature or extent of the censure, but in the matter of absolution. Formerly reserved to the Ordinary, the absolution from this censure is now further restricted, being reserved to the Apostolic See *simpliciter*. One reason for this change may appear from the fact that a new censure has been incorporated into

2 C. 8, D. XXVIII; c. 5, 9, D. XXVIII; c. 1, C. XX, q. 3.
3 C. 4, 5 C., XXVII, q. 1.
4 C. un. de consang., IV, in Clem.

the general law,[5] and affects certain religious of either sex who are excluded from the law now under discussion, i. e., those who have taken simple, perpetual vows. Since it has been deemed proper to reserve the new censure, and since the general principle of proportion in penalties with respect to the delinquencies is followed by the Legislator, the censure incurred by clerics in Sacred Orders and those having solemn vows is reserved to the Holy See, the other censure only to the Ordinary. (Can. 2388, 2.)

The offence which here merits excommunication is consummated when the marriage is attempted, even though the marriage is null by reason of the impediment of Sacred Orders,[6] or the profession of solemn vows,[7] or any other impediment.[8] Moreover, the Holy Office has declared, and the decision is now confirmed by the Code, that the censure is incurred even by the attempt at civil marriage.[9]

Presumption is required, as heretofore, for incurring the penalty, and hence any ignorance, even though it be crass or supine, of fact or of law, excuses from the censure. It is probably not incurred if the parties, after their ignorance has been dispelled, continue to cohabit.[10] Full and true matrimonial consent must also be had, for it is the mutual consent that makes the marriage, and if the marriage is null for want of consent the offense is not a complete one and hence is not punishable with a censure. Hence if either party or both acted in substantial error, or under grave fear, or merely simulated the matrimonial consent, neither can be said to have incurred the censure here concerned.[11]

Although the Scholastics of the Society of Jesus take

5 See Art. VI of this chapter.

6 Can. 1072.

7 Can. 1073.

8 Decr. S. C. S. Off., Jan. 13, 1892.

9 Dec. 22, 1880.

10 Lehmkuhl, "Theol. Mor." Ed. 4, 1887, II, p. 689; Bonacina, l. c., D. 2, qu. 4, p. 7, n. 18; Can. 2229.

11 Cann. 2229, 1083, 1086, 1087; cf. Sanchez, "De Matr." VII, 48, nn. 10-12.

only simple vows, these vows, nevertheless, in virtue of a concession granted the Society by Gregory XIII,[12] constitute a diriment impediment to marriage, so that in this respect these persons are in the same class as those of solemn vows. However, this does not bring them under the present law inflicting a censure, for they do not, properly speaking, take solemn vows.

II. Const. *Apost. Sedis:*

"Procurantes abortum, effectu secuto."

Codex I.C., 2350:

"Procurantes abortum, matre non excepta, incurrunt, effectu secuto, in excommunicationem latae sententiae Ordinario reservatam; . . ."

Abortion is the illicit ejection of an immature fetus from the womb of the mother.[13] A common practice and often commended among the Greeks and the Romans, it has always been considered a heinous crime by the Church. As early as the year 314 its condemnation had become "ancient."[14] (Council of Ancyra, Can. 21.) Pope Stephen V (816-817), in a letter to Bishop Humbert of Mainz, condemned as a homicide the woman who destroys her fetus. Innocent II, in 1211, held as equally guilty those who give cause to abortion, and suspended all ecclesiastics guilty of the crime.

The censure of excommunication, as a punishment of this crime, was first imposed by Sixtus V. In virtue of the Const. *Effraenatam,* Oct. 9, 1588, this censure, reserved specially to the Roman Pontiff, was incurred *ipso facto* by all who caused the abortion of a fetus animate or inanimate, the mother likewise included. This severe measure, however, did not retard the spread of the deplorable practice. Women procured abortion to avoid shame, and, lest their sins be discovered, refrained from

12 Const. *Ascendente Domino,* May 25, 1584; cf. Can. 1058, 2.

13 "Immature"—before the beginning of the seventh month of gestation. Capellman, "Medicina Pastoralis," Aquisgrani, 1910, n. 10; Antonelli, "Med. Pastor." Romae, 1920, II, n. 74 ss.

14 Eschbach, "Disputationes Physiologico-Theologicae," ed. 3, Romae, Disp. III, p. 78.

seeking the absolution, now difficult to obtain, and remained in their sin.[15] In the interest of souls Gregory XIV modified the Sistine legislation[16] so as to be co-extensive with that of the Council of Trent,[17] exempting the mother from the censure and excluding the abortion of an *inanimate* fetus. Besides, absolution from the censure was no longer reserved to the Roman Pontiff, but rather to bishops.

Other changes appear in the renewal of the censure by Pius IX in 1869. Co-operators in the crime are no longer mentioned, and no distinction is made between animate and inanimate fetuses. Again, the censure was inflicted upon "procurantes abortum," which seemed to be a reversion to the classification of Sixtus V: "qui foetus ejectionem . . . procuraverint." Whether Pius IX had this intention has been much controverted by canonists and moralists, since upon this depended the exemption of the mother under the law of 1869.[18] The controversy is definitely settled with the promulgation of the new Code, in which the mother is expressly declared to be liable to the censure.

III. Const. *Apost. Sedis:*

> "Litteris Apostolicae Sedis falsis scienter utentes vel crimini in ea re co-operantes."

Codex I.C., Can. 2360:

> "Omnes fabricatores vel falsarii litterarum, decretorum vel rescriptorum Sedis Apostolicae vel iisdem litteris, decretis vel rescriptis scienter utentes incurrunt ipso facto in excommunicationem speciali modo Sedi Apostolicae reservatam."

15 Wernz, VI, n. 360 ss.

16 Const. *Sedis Apostolicae,* May 31, 1591.

17 Sess. XIV, cap. 7, de ref.

18 Each side of this question has had worthy protagonists. The exemption of the mother was defended by such able authorities as Bellerini-Palmieri, "Theol. Moral.," n. 320; Lehmkuhl, n. 970; Noldin, "De Poenis," n. 93; Vecchiotti, "Instit. Canon." II, 363; Lega, "Praelect. I. C.," n. 55; Pennachi, l. c., II, p. 42; Nouv. Revue Theol., T. XI, p. 320. The contrary opinion was upheld by Bucceroni, "Const. Apost. Sedis," n. 79; D'Annibale, l. c., n. 161; Genicot, "Theol. Moral." I, n. 608; Wernz, VI, n. 370; etc.

To avoid undue repetition we may refer here to what was said in Chap. I, Art. IX, regarding the extent of the term "Apostolic Letters" in the old law and the express mention of "decrees" and "rescripts" in the new Code. In the present article we need only to observe that the law of Pius IX, as regards the use of these documents, has been confirmed in the newly promulgated law.

One important change occurs. The censure of excommunication, which heretofore was reserved to the Ordinary, is now assimilated to that incurred by fabricators and falsifiers of the Apostolic documents and is reserved in a special manner to the Holy See. The new reservation is the more logical. For the use of spurious or falsified letters constitutes no less injury to the Holy See than the very fabrication or mutilation of Apostolic Letters; indeed, the evil effect of falsification is chiefly produced when the letters are put to use and the illicit orders which they contain executed.

IV. Notwithstanding the severe penalties with which Pope Pius IX punished trafficking in Mass stipends,[19] his measures did not succeed in uprooting the detestable practice. Booksellers and merchants continued to organize public collections of stipends and retain the money as payment for books, wines, etc., which they delivered to the clergy, who would complete the bargain by saying the required Masses. The warning of the Sacred Congr. of the Council on July 25, 1874, was of no avail. Leo XIII, determined to eliminate the practice, declared, in the Const. *Vigilanti studio,* that clerics in sacred Orders engaging in the nefarious traffic should incur *ipso facto* suspension *a divinis* reserved to the Holy See; other clerics irregularity, and laymen excommunication reserved to the Ordinary. The law was later extended to the Eastern Church and was confirmed by Pius X.[20]

The censure of excommunication in the present case no longer exists. Having taken its rise from a particular

19 Cf. Chap. II, Art. XII.

20 Coll. P. F., n. 1847; Const. *Ut debita,* May 11, 1904.

abuse of the times, it is now deemed unnecessary, particularly in the form of a *latae sententiae* punishment. The abuse which brought it about is, indeed, as severely condemned today as it was by Leo XIII,[21] and penalties *ferendae sententiae* are provided for offenders.[22] The censure of excommunication may still be incurred by the layman who engages in the reprobated practice, as is evident from Can. 2324.

V. Codex I.C., Can. 2326:

> **"Qui falsas reliquias conficit, aut scienter vendit, distribuit vel publicae fidelium venerationi exponit, ipso facto excommunicationem Ordinario reservatam contrahit."**

It has been the constant mind of the Church that only true relics, duly authenticated and determined, shall be exposed for public veneration on the part of the faithful. Thus, Pope Innocent III, in the Fourth Lateran Council (1215), forbade that newly discovered relics be accorded public veneration until they had been approved by the authority of the Roman Pontiff.[23] According to a decree of the Council of Trent, new relics, before they are received for public veneration, must be examined and approved by the Bishop, who is urged to seek the advice of theologians and other competent men in order to appraise the true worth of the relics.[24] Clement IX in 1669 created the new *"Congregation of Indulgences and Sacred Relics,"* to which he entrusted the official authentication of sacred remains. We may also recall here that Pius V, in 1613, in order to prevent the distribution of spurious relics, pronounced excommunication *latae sententiae* upon those who removed the remains of the Saints and Martyrs from the Roman Catacombs and cemeteries.

Finally we have in the Code the reaffirmation of the Tridentine decree that only those relics can be publicly

21 Codex I. C., Lib. III, Tit. III, Art. 4.

22 Can. 2324.

23 C. 2, X, de reliquiis, III, 45.

24 Sess. XXV, de invocatione, etc.

worshipped whose genuineness is vouched for by an authentic document signed by a Cardinal, the Local Ordinary, or some other ecclesiastic authorized by Apostolic indult to authenticate relics.[25] Besides this, there now exists a censure of excommunication reserved to the Ordinary and incurred *ipso facto* by those who make false relics, or who knowingly sell, distribute or expose them to the public veneration of the faithful.[26] The censure, being new, requires some comment.

The relics here referred to are those of the Saints and, *a fortiori,* Our Blessed Savior. These would include, for example, the sacred bodies, or parts thereof, as the head, arm, hand, finger, bone, teeth, hair, ashes, etc.; likewise garments which the Saints wore or in which they were buried, and also instruments used in their martyrdom, as the cross, sword, chains, etc.

Four classes of persons are liable to the censure: (a) those who manufacture false relics; for example, one who would enclose a piece of common wood, or bone, or cloth, in a case, to simulate a sacred relic; (b) those who, knowing that a relic is spurious, sell it, openly or secretly, as an authenticated relic; (c) those who, although not asking a price for the false relic, yet offer it to another as a relic duly approved by ecclesiastical authority; (d) those who formally expose, e. g., in public procession, false relics for the public veneration of the faithful. It must be noted that the censure is not incurred unless full knowledge and deliberate consent are had by those who sell, distribute or expose the false relics, which implies that they know the relics are false and know also that the sale, distribution or exposition of the same is forbidden under pain of excommunication.

VI. In Article I of the present Chapter we discussed the censure of excommunication, reserved to the Holy See, which is incurred by clerics in Sacred Orders and religious who have taken the solemn vow of chastity if they attempt to marry, and by all who attempt to con-

25 Can. 1283, 1.
26 Can. cit.

tract marriage with these persons. (Can. 2388.) That censure, while it has been of long standing, has always been restricted to those religious who have taken the solemn vows. The Code of 1918, however, contains a new censure which affects those of simple, perpetual vows. Thus,

Can. 2388, 2:

> "Quodsi sint professi votorum simplicium perpetuorum, tam in Ordinibus quam in Congregationibus religiosis, omnes, uti supra (scl. et professos ipsos et eos qui cum iisdem matrimonium etiam civiliter tantum contrahere praesumunt), excommunicatio tenet latae sententiae Ordinario reservata."

Simple vows, while they impede the contraction of marriage, do not constitute a diriment impediment. (Can. 1058.) Hence the marriage of religious in simple vows is valid, unless null for some other reason, but is unlawful and sinful because it exposes the person to the danger of violating his vow and implies the intention to consummate the marriage, whereby the vow is violated.[27] We see, therefore, the wisdom of the Legislator in imposing the censure not only upon the religious, but also upon those with whom they contract.

In religion the new censure may be contracted by sisters whose simple vows are also perpetual; by nuns whose vows are by their rule solemn, but for certain territories have been declared simple by the Holy See; by those who take simple perpetual vows in a Religious Congregation or in an Order. Outside of religion the censure is incurred by anyone who contracts marriage, even civil, with any of these persons.

For all concerned the excommunication is reserved to the Ordinary. Absolution can therefore be granted to any one by his own Ordinary and even to *peregrini* by the Ordinary of the place where they happen to be. (Can. 2253, 3.)

27 Can. 1058, 2388.

VII. Codex I.C., Can. 2385:

> "Firmo praescripto can. 646, religiosus, apostata a religione, ipso jure incurrit in excommunicationem, proprio Superiori majori vel, si religio sit laicalis aut non exempta, Ordinario loci in quo commoratur, reservatam, . . ."

Since the fourth century the ideal religious life has been that of perpetual perseverance in the religious state.[28] The Council of Trent obliged bishops to punish as apostates religious who returned to the world, and to demand their return to their monasteries.[29]

By the common law in force before Pentecost of 1918 the censure of excommunication for apostasy from religion was *ferendae sententiae,* being inflicted by the competent ecclesiastical Superior. In virtue of a decree of Boniface VIII excommunication was incurred *ipso facto* by apostate religious when they laid aside their religious habit, but the penalty was abrogated implicitly by subsequent decrees,[30] and the practice of the *Congregation of Bishops and Regulars* in obliging apostates from religion to cease wearing the habit.

The censure, then, contained in Can. 2385 is newly introduced. It is incurred only by "apostates from religion" in the canonical sense—those who, after taking perpetual vows, solemn or simple, unlawfully leave the religious house with the purpose of not returning; or who, having lawfully left the house, remain outside with the intention of withdrawing themselves thereby from the religious obedience. The malicious intent is presumed by law if the religious does not within one month return to the house or declare to the superior his intention of returning.[31] It is also provided in the law that a male religious who flees with a woman, or a female religious with a man,

28 C. 69, D. L.; C. 1-3, C. XX, q. 3.

29 Sess. XXV, c. 19.

30 C. 2, ne clerici, III, 24, in Sexto; Clem. VIII, May 26, 1593; Urban VIII, Sept. 21, 1624; Conc. Trid. Sess. XXV, c. 19, de reg.; cf. Wernz, n. 276 ss.

31 Can. 644.

is by that very fact considered as legitimately dismissed. (Can. 646, I, 2.)

It must be observed that the presumption of the apostate's intention of not returning or of withdrawing himself from religious obedience is only a "'praesumptio juris," and is founded on the failure of the religious to return within a month or at least to give promise of returning. If, therefore, the religious brings proof that he did not have the "malicious intent," or that he was unable to return or to send word to the superior, or that he wrote a letter, which was not received or was mislaid, then the presumption yields, there is no apostasy, and the censure cannot be enforced.

The censure is reserved to the Ordinary, and might have been so stated. But Can. 2385 applies the distinction, as to the proper Ordinary, between exempt and non-exempt religious. Hence it declares that the censure, if incurred by a member of an exempt clerical religion, is reserved to the major Superior[32] of that religion, while that incurred by a member of a lay or non-exempt religion is reserved to the Ordinary of the place where the delinquent happens to be. This is the application of Can. 198.[33]

Capello, commenting upon this censure, suggests that it may be doubted whether nuns and sisters are comprehended by this law. The reason for the doubt is that "lay religious" is here used as distinguished from "clerical," which consists of men only. The doubt, however, seems hardly justifiable. For the lay religion is indeed distinguished from the clerical, which, being defined as a religion whose members generally are ordained to the priesthood,[34] implies that any religion in which this def-

32 Cf. Can. 488, 8.

33 A religion is clerical if most of its members are ordained to the priesthood, as the Order of Preachers, Society of Jesus, etc; but if its members cannot be ordained, as e. g., a female institute, or by their Constitution do not seek ordination, it is known as a lay religion.

34 Can. 488, 4.

inition is not verified is a lay religion and therefore comprehends female religious.[35]

VIII. Codex I.C., Can. 2319:

> I. "Subsunt excommunicationi latae sententiae Ordinario reservatae catholicae:
>
> 1. Qui matrimonium ineunt coram ministro acatholico contra praescriptum can. 1063, 1;
> 2. Qui matrimonio uniuntur cum pacto explicito vel implicito ut omnis vel aliqua proles educetur extra catholicam Ecclesiam;
> 3. Qui scienter liberos suos acatholicis ministris baptizandos offerre praesumunt;
> 4. Parentes vel parentum locum tenentes qui liberos in religione acatholica educandos vel instituendos scienter tradunt."

A. In the general law we now have for the first time an explicit excommunication for the favor which is shown to heresy when a Catholic contracts marriage before a non-Catholic minister. It is true such offenders have long been considered as "accomplices of heretics" and have incurred the penalties of heretics, among which is excommunication reserved in a special manner to the Holy See.[36] It was thought that this ruling was abrogated by Pius IX when he failed to specify the case in the Const. *Apost. Sedis,* but subsequent decrees gave assurance that the offense was punishable as heresy.[37]

Today the censure is inflicted specifically upon those Catholics who contract marriage before a non-Catholic minister acting as such. The law is measured by Can. 1063, 1, the violation of which constitutes the offense to which the excommunication is attached. In that canon we read: Even when a dispensation from the impediment of Mixed Religion (or Disparity of Worship, in virtue of Can. 1071) has been obtained from the Church, the parties cannot, either before or after their marriage in the Church, go also, whether personally or through

35 Cf. Cavigioli, l. c., n. 164; Chelodi, l. c., n. 101; Cerato, l. c., n. 73.

36 S. C. S. Off. Mar. 7, 1842, Feb. 17, 1864.

37 S. C. S. Off. Mar. 17, 1874, May 11, 1892.

a representative, to a non-Catholic minister acting as such, to give or to renew the matrimonial consent.

But we must here take into consideration that the Third Plenary Council of Baltimore also enacted legislation on the question of marriage of Catholics before a non-Catholic minister.[38] That Council decreed that those Catholics who contract marriage before a minister of any non-Catholic sect incur excommunication *latae sententiae* reserved to any Ordinary or to the delinquent's own Ordinary, according as one appeared before the non-Catholic minister outside or within one's own diocese. A question arises, therefore, as to the abrogation of the censure instituted by the Council of Baltimore. Certainly, if we look upon the general law (Can. 2319, 1, 1) and the particular law (Baltimore) as contemplating different *delicta* we must conclude that the Baltimore censure is still in force. (Can. 6, 1.) And even if the Code contemplates the same case as the law of Baltimore, namely, the giving or renewal of the matrimonial consent before a non-Catholic minister acting as such, yet it does not readily appear that the Baltimore censure is abrogated.[39] For, the laws of the Baltimore Council, being particular laws, remain in force in so far as they are not opposed to the Code. (Can. 6, 1.)[40] Moreover, Paragraph 5 of Canon 6, which declares that all penalties not mentioned in the Code are abrogated, refers to penalties contained in the general, not the particular laws.

In Can. 2244, 2, we read: "Censura latae sententiae multiplicatur: . . . 3. Si delictum, *diversis censuris* a distinctis Superioribus punitum, semel aut pluries committatur." Perhaps we may infer from this[41] that if the

38 "Acta Concilii Plenarii Balt. III, n. 127.

39 Cf. Chelodi, "Jus Matrimoniale," n. 62; Cerato, "Censurae vigentes," n. 69, d; Caviglioli, "Censurae Latae Sententiae," n. 155; Augustine, op. cit., Vol. V, p. 150; Ayrinhac, "Marriage Legislation in the New Code of Canon Law," n. 213.

40 For this reason the other excommunication instituted by the Third Plenary Council is still in force, namely, the excommunication reserved to the Ordinary and incurred *ipso facto* by those who dare to attempt marriage after having obtained a civil divorce.

41 Thus Chelodi, o. c. n. 32, not. 4.

same offense is punished in common law and in particular with the censures specifically the same, v. g., two excommunications, then the person who commits that offense incurs only the censure inflicted by the common law. To apply this interpretation in the present case, the Catholic who contracts a mixed marriage before a non-Catholic minister acting as such incurs the excommunication contained in Can. 2319, but not that enacted by the Baltimore Council. This supposes that "diversis censuris" means censures specifically different. If, however, it means censures different in the sense that they are imposed by distinct superiors, it follows that, in our case, two censures are incurred, both of which must be mentioned when absolution is sought. (Can. 2249, 2.)

Strict interpretation[42] requires that the censure contained in Can. 2319 be restricted to those Catholics who contract marriage with non-Catholics, since this appears to be the extent of Can. 1063, 1, the violation of which constitutes the delictum in the present case. Hence, two Catholics who attempt marriage before a non-Catholic minister would not incur this censure,[43] although they would incur the censure imposed by the Council of Baltimore, which admits of no such restrictions.

The Baltimore law restricted absolution to the proper Ordinary of the delinquents if they contracted the marriage in their own diocese. This restriction, however, can no longer be sustained. For there is question here of a *reservatio a jure in particulari territorio,* and hence we must apply Canon 2247, 2, which says: "Reservatio censurae in particulari territorio vim suam extra illius territorii fines non exserit, etiamsi censuratus ad absolutionem obtinendam e territorio egrediatur." The Baltimore censure, then, if it be incurred, is simply reserved to the Ordinary.

Certain delinquencies to which mixed marriages have given rise are now punished with excommunication reserved likewise to the Ordinary:

42 Cf. Cann. 19, 2219, 3.

43 Cf. Chelodi, l. c., n. 60; Cavigioli, l. c., n. 155.

B. When the Church grants a dispensation from the impediment of Disparity of Worship or of Mixed Religion she always does so on condition that the contracting parties promise to have all their children baptized and educated in the Catholic Church. Moreover, it must be morally certain that these promises will be fulfilled.[44] This is a safeguard which the Church deems necessary for the future welfare of the children. It is no small crime, then, for a Catholic to attempt to defeat the wise purpose of the Church by entering matrimony with the understanding, even only implicit, that one or more of the children shall be reared outside the Church. Such an act is now punished with the severe penalty of excommunication, which is incurred not when the unlawful agreement is entered, but when the marriage is contracted by the parties so agreeing. The agreement must exist at the time of the marriage. Hence the censure would not be incurred if the agreement was annulled by either party before the marriage took place, nor if the agreement was made only after the marriage.

C. Another act favorable to heresy and now punished with excommunication reserved to the Ordinary is that of parents who knowingly have their children baptized by non-Catholic ministers. This, again, is in violation of the promises which the Church exacts of the parties to a mixed marriage.

The penalty is not incurred in case of urgent necessity, nor if the parent act without full knowledge and deliberation, as, for example, not knowing that the minister is a non-Catholic, or that the Church prohibits this particular act, or even that there is a censure attached to the action. This ignorance, even when crass or supine, exempts one from the censure. (Cf. Can. 2229.)

The censure affects only the parents, legitimate or natural, of the children presented for the unlawful baptism, which excludes the other members of the family and

44 Can. 1061, 1071.

friends, neighbors, servants, *locum tenentes,* etc. Moreover, the offense is not completed, and hence the excommunication not contracted, unless the non-Catholic minister performed the ceremony of baptizing the child. It matters not here, it seems, whether the sacrament is validly or invalidly conferred, for the penalty is intended to prevent and punish the unlawful communication with heretics and schismatics, rather than the exposing of the child to invalid baptism.[45]

D. Finally, excommunication likewise reserved to the Ordinary is incurred by parents and persons holding the place of parents, who knowingly hand over a child in their charge to be brought up or educated in a non-Catholic sect. Here, again, we deal with an act favorable to heresy. In fact, offenders in this case, as well as those mentioned under B and C, are by law suspected of heresy.[46]

The law does not here specify "liberos suos" as it does in the preceding censure, because persons who are not true parents are also comprehended by the law. A child cannot be "handed over" in the present sense except by one who has the authority of a parent over the child. Such authority is enjoyed by parents over their own children and also by guardians, tutors and heads of families who have taken children under their parental care by legal adoption or by way of temporary provision, or even by a commission from the State. Such guardians, tutors, curators, etc., would be *locum tenentes* of the true parents and assume the responsibility of the Catholic parents to have the children brought up according to the will of the Catholic Church.

"Educare" signifies to form or foster by nurturing, as is done by nurses and others who first have charge of the training of young children. "Instituere" generally signifies to teach, to instruct youths—to establish them in a way of thinking and acting and living. Hence an "institute" is understood as a school or place where such teach-

45 Cf. Cavigioli, l. c., n. 157; Reg. 15, 23, 49, R. J. in Sexto.
46 Can. 2319, 2.

ing or instruction is performed by higher educators rather than by nurses, etc.[47] To place, then, a child in charge of a nurse, tutor or teacher who will mould or instruct the child according to a non-Catholic religion, or to entrust it to a home, school, or institute, even by daily attendance only, which the Catholic parent or guardian knows will educate the child in a religion other than the Catholic—any of these acts, if done with full knowledge and deliberation, merits excommunication reserved to the Ordinary.

47 Cf. Forcellini, Lexicon, s. v. "Educo," "Instituo"; Cerato, l. c., n. 69.

CHAPTER IV

EXCOMMUNICATIONS UNRESERVED

The fourth and last series of excommunications contained in the Constitution *Apostolicae Sedis* is that of excommunications which were incurred *ipso facto,* but were not reserved, either to the Roman Pontiff or to Ordinaries, and from which, therefore, absolution could be obtained in the Sacramental forum from any approved confessor, and in the external forum from anyone who had jurisdiction in the external forum.[1] The Constitution contains four such censures, which we shall here compare with the legislation of today. Besides these we must treat eight censures of this nature and extent enacted by the Council of Trent, which have, in virtue of the Const. *Apost Sedis* continued in force until the new Code was promulgated, and of which two find confirmation in the Code itself. Finally we shall consider a censure of excommunication that was enacted by Pope Urban VIII in 1633, abrogated implicitly by Pius IX in 1869 and later revived by the latter.

To quote the words of the Const. *Apostolicae Sedis:*

> "Excommunicationi latae sententiae nemini reservatae subjacere declaramus:
>
> I. "Mandantes seu cogentes tradi ecclesiasticae sepulturae haereticos notorios aut nominatim excommunicatos vel interdictos."

Codex I.C., Can. 2339:

> "Qui ausi fuerint mandare seu cogere tradi ecclesiasticae sepulturae infideles, apostatas a fide, vel haereticos, schismaticos, aliosve sive excommunicatos sive interdictos contra praescriptum can. 1240, 1, contrahunt excommunicationem latae sententiae nemini reservatam."

1 Can. 2253, 1. Wernz, o. c. VI, 175.

Since in life Christians are temples of the Holy Ghost and are intimately associated with Christ in Baptism, the Most Blessed Eucharist and the other Sacraments, the Church has always desired that their bodies, after death, be kept apart from those of unbelievers.[2] In fact, She has provided that the places where the bodies of Catholics are buried shall be places specially blessed for that purpose.[3]

Certain classes of persons have long been denied burial in such places. Pope Innocent III in the Fourth Lateran Council (1215) forbade clerics under pain of losing their ecclesiastical offices, to grant Christian burial to heretics or to those who had been excommunicated or placed under interdict *nominatim.*[4] By a decree of Alexander IV (1254-61) excommunication was incurred *ipso facto* by those who knowingly gave Christian burial to heretics or those who believe, receive, defend or favor heretics, absolution from the censure being denied until the delinquent had publicly and with his own hands removed the body unlawfully buried.[5] Clement V, in the Council of Vienne (1312), enacted the same censure for those who knowingly bury persons publicly excommunicated, interdicted by name or manifest usurers.[6]

In 1869 Pius IX tempered the ancient law, restricting it to the burial of only notorious heretics and those excommunicated or interdicted *nominatim.* Moreover, not those who bury, but those who command or force others to bury the prohibited persons were thenceforth liable to the censure.

The new law retains the censure and leaves it unreserved. It restricts the offense, however, to "presumptuous" action ("Qui ausi feurint"), so that today fear or ignorance, even though this be crass or supine, excuses one from the censure.[7] The "mandantes" and "cogentes"

2 C. 22, C. XIII, q. 2.
3 Rit. Rom. Tit. II, c. 1; Tit. VI, c. 1; Tit. VIII, c. 29.
4 C. 13, 24, X, de haereticis, V, 7.
5 C. 2, de haereticis, V, 2, in Sexto.
6 C. 1, de sepulturis, III, 7, in Clem.
7 Can. 2229, 2.

are those who, acting by public authority vested in them, as e. g., the Governor, Mayor, Sheriff, etc., order or command or force those in charge of cemeteries to give ecclesiastical burial to a person denied the right by Can. 1240, 1.[8]

As regards the offenses to which the present censure is attached, the former law has been considerably extended, since the denial of Christian burial has now a wider extent. Formerly this censure was restricted to the burial of notorious heretics and those excommunicated or interdicted "nominatim." In virtue of Can. 1240, 1, which now measures the extent of the burials forbidden under pain of censure, we must add to those already named: (a) notorious apostates from the faith, notorious schismatics and those notoriously attached to the "Masons" or other such organizations that militate against Church and State; (b) suicides (deliberate); (c) those who have died in duels or from wounds received therein; (d) those who have ordered their bodies to be cremated; and (e) other public and manifest sinners. It must be remarked that none of these may be denied ecclesiastical burial if before death they have given any sign of repentance. Heretofore those who died as the result of duelling, even if they gave signs of repentance and had been absolved, were denied Christian burial. The other classes of persons just mentioned are not now excluded for the first time,[9] but it is only since the promulgation of the Code that the excommunication is incurred by commanding or forcing their burial in consecrated ground.

Finally, a question arises as to the meaning of "ecclesiastical burial" in this connection. The present article of the Const. *Apost. Sedis* was generally understood to apply even in those cases in which the mere burial in consecrated ground was obtained forcibly or by command, regardless of the performance of the sacred rites, but not

8 D'Annibale, l. c., n. 167; Noldin, "De Poenis," n. 97; Bonacina, Disp. II, Qu. II, P. II, n. 2: "Cogere idem est ac per vim vel metum gravem injuste inducere."

9 Rit. Rom. Tit. VI, c. 2, n. 8.

vice versa.[10] Accordingly, if we now retain the former interpretation,[11] as several recent commentators would recommend,[12] "ecclesiastical burial," as used in Can. 2339, is to be understood in the sense that burial in consecrated ground, without the transferring of the body to the church or the performance therein of the sacred rites, is sufficient (provided it be maliciously forced or commanded) to constitute the offence to which the censure of excommunication is attached. However, we are here dealing with penalties and must not lose sight of the principle: "Odiosa sunt restringenda." The pre-Code interpretation of this law, which held that the mere burial was sufficient matter for the censure, was, no doubt, justified, inasmuch as this constituted true "ecclesiastical burial." But the Legislator now states formally, in Can. 1204, what the Church understands by "ecclesiastical burial," and we may justly assume that, when the term is used throughout the Code, it is used in the sense of this definition. Therefore, it seems only proper to conclude that unless the three conditions named in Can. 1204 are verified one cannot, however sinful and reprehensible his action, be said to have ordered or forced the unlawful granting of ecclesiastical burial, and, hence, cannot be said to have incurred the present censure.[13]

II. Const. *Apost. Sedis:*

> "Laedentes et perterrefacientes Inquisitores, denuntiantes, testes, aliosve ministros S. Officii, ejusve sacrae tribunalis scripturas deripientes, aut comburentes, vel praedictis quibuslibet auxilium, consilium, favorem praestantes."

10 Bucceroni, "Comment. in Const. A. S.," n. 84; D'Annibale, l. c., n. 167; Tephany, l. c., n. 422; Pennachi, l. c., II, p. 67; Lehmkuhl, l. c., II, n. 972; Wernz, VI, n. 192.

11 Can. 6, 3.

12 Cf. Noldin, l. c., n. 97; Pighi, "De Censuris," n. 81; Sole, "De Delictis et Poenis" 367.

13 Can. 19. This interpretation is supported by several recent Commentators: Chelodi, l. c., n. 73; Cerato, n. 63; Capello, n. 137; Cavigioli, n. 170.

Although the Bishops of the Church have always been charged with the duty of searching out heresy and guarding the faithful from its infection, yet it is only after the great upheaval caused by the heresiarch Luther that the Congregation known as the "Roman and Universal Inquisition"[14] was established[15] to be the final court of appeals for trials concerning faith, and the court of first instance for cases reserved to the Roman Pontiff. In their work the Inquisitors often were hampered by laymen who, setting up their private judgment against that of the Inquisitors, would seek to mitigate or to aggravate penalties imposed by these officials, or to obstruct the execution of their sentences.[16] It was to protect the Sacred Inquisitors from such interference and to insure the efficacy of their decrees that Paul V, by the Const. *Si de protegendis,*[17] instituted the censure of excommunication cited above. Pius IX, in 1869, renewed the censure, but restricted its extent somewhat. Thus, injuring Bishops in the exercise of their office, the invasion of churches, houses, etc., of the Inquisitors, attacking the prison of the Holy Office, releasing prisoners, etc.—these acts were no longer comprehended by the law.

The censure itself was retained by Pius IX rather to reassert a principle than as a measure required by the latter times. It is omitted entirely from the new Code, which, however, provides punishment for injurious attacks, direct or indirect, against the Sacred Congregations in the public press, speeches, etc., and for actions calculated to excite animosity against their acts, decrees, decisions and sentences. The penalties are *ferendae sententiae* and are left to the judgment of the Ordinary.[18]

III. Const. *Apost. Sedis:*

> "Alienantes et recipere praesumentes bona ecclesiastica absque beneplacito Apostolico ad for-

14 Later the Congregation of the Holy Office.
15 Paul III, Const. *Licet ab initio,* July 21, 1542.
16 Cf. Const. *Licet a diversis,* Julius III, Feb. 14, 1551.
17 April 1, 1569.
18 Can. 2344.

> mam Extravagantis 'Ambitiosae' de rebus ecclesiasticis non alienandis."

Codex I.C., Can. 2347:

> "Firma nullitate actus et obligatione, etiam per censuram urgenda, restituendi bona illegitime acquisita ac reparandi damna forte illata, qui bona ecclesiastica alienare praesumpserit aut in alienandis consensum praebere contra praescripta can. 534, 1, et can. 1532. . . .
>
> 3. . . . si beneplacitum apistolicum, in memoratis canonibus praescriptum, fuerit scienter praetermissum, omnes quovis modo reos sive recipiendo sive consensum praebendo, manet praeterea excommunicatio latae sententiae nemini reservata."

Although the arbitrary alienation of ecclesiastical goods was forbidden in the very earliest days of the Church,[19] the censure with which we are here concerned dates back to the pontificate of Paul II (1464-1471). To eradicate certain abuses to which the property of the Church was being subjected he pronounced, in the Const. *Ambitiosae*[20] excommunication to be incurred *ipso facto* by any one who would, without the permission of the Apostolic See, alienate any goods belonging to the Church, the alienation itself remaining invalid. This Constitution was not accepted very generally outside of Italy, especially in France, Belgium and Germany, where a contrary custom prevailed, although the Roman Congregations several times declared the Constitution was to be observed.[21]

Pius IX, in the Const. *Apost. Sedis*, forbade alienation according to the prescription of the Const. *Ambitiosae*, and, since the censures contained in the former were promulgated as for the first time, the censure enacted by Paul II was thenceforth to apply entirely and universally.[22]

19 C. 12, C. XII, q. 2.

20 Mar. 1, 1468.

21 Cf. Reiffenst. Lib. III, T. XIII; Schmalzgr. Lib. III, Tit. XIII; S. C. C. Nov. 15, 1655; Mar. 14, 1682.

22 Cf. Wernz, III, n. 165.

The Code also requires, within certain limits, the permission of the Holy See in this matter.[23] Under the present law also alienation without due permission is invalid and restitution must be made and can be demanded, even under pain of censure.[24]

Can. 2347 forbids under pain of excommunication the alienation, not of all ecclesiastical goods as was forbidden by the Const. *Ambitiosae*, but those of certain classes and values. However, the requirements of Paul II were mitigated even before the Code. By a decree of the S. Cong. de Propaganda Fide, dated Sept. 25, 1885, the bishops of the United States, on account of the peculiar circumstance here obtaining, were dispensed *ad decennium* from the solemnities required by the Const. *Apost. Sedis*, which faculties have been renewed every ten years. The faculties were to be used cautiously and with the advice of the Diocesan Consultors; and the Congregation required a triennial report of the use of the faculties and of the several dioceses in which they were used.[25] The Fathers of the Third Plenary Council of Baltimore declared that papal permission and the consent of the Diocesan Consultors was required for the valid alienation of property whose value exceeded five thousand dollars ($5,000).[26]

Compared with the Const. *Ambitiosae* and the Const. *Apostolicae Sedis*, the law of the Code allows considerable freedom in this matter. And yet it is substantially the discipline which has been in force in the United States since the Third Plenary Council of Baltimore, although the solemnities required by the Code are arranged according to the divers classes and values of ecclesiastical goods. However, our Bishops are now to enjoy greater latitude in this regard, for, in virtue of the Decree of the

23 The reasonableness of the restriction is readily seen. For, while the dominion of ecclesiastical goods belongs to the moral person who has legally acquired them, this dominion is held under the Supreme Authority of the Apostolic See. Can. 1499, 2.

24 Can. 2347.

25 Acta Conc. Plen. Balt. III, pag. ciii.

26 Acta, n. 20.

Sacred Consistorial Congregation, dated March 17, 1922, the Bishops of the United States and Canada can obtain, from the Sacred Congregation of the Council, faculties for permitting the alienation of ecclesiastical goods to the sum of ten thousand dollars ($10,000), and the Bishops of South America and other regions to the sum of fifteen thousand (15,000) pesos. These faculties are to be used only in case of necessity and when there is not sufficient time for recourse to the Holy See. Moreover, the Holy See must be notified immediately upon the completion of the alienation.[27]

The punishment for unlawful alienation of goods which require an apostolic indult is still excommunication unreserved. The actions prohibited under pain of censure are "alienation" and the corresponding "reception," presumption being required in each case. The meaning of "alienation" is not quite clear. The former law, taking as its norm the Const. *Ambitiosae,* was rightly held by authors to comprehend the various contracts which the dominion, usufructs or rights belonging to the Church were transferred and conceded to another person, physical or moral. Hence "alienation" included not only the contracts of "emptio et venditio," but also "donatio," "locatio et conductio ultra triennium," "infeudatio," "emphyteusis," and all such contracts by which the condition of the Church was impaired.[28] It may be doubted, however, whether the present law imposing excommunication affects any action other than "alienation" properly so-called and the corresponding acceptance. For the censure is levied in Can. 2347 upon those who presume to alienate property without observing certain formalities required by Canons 534, 1 and 1532. Can. 534, 1 contains provision for the alienation of goods of religious communities. Can. 1532 specifies the solemnities required according to the nature and the value of the property. And, while the solemnities

27 Decret. cit. III, n. 5.

28 Cf. D'Annibale, l. c., n. 175; Pennachi, II, p. 115 ss.; Wernz, III, n. 154 ss.

are also, in Can. 1533, made essential to all other contracts in which the condition of the Church is impaired, yet this Canon (1533) is not alleged in Can. 2347, and hence cannot demand observance under pain of censure.[29] On the other hand, Can. 1533 can be construed as merely elaborating the extent of Can. 1532 so as to confirm the former and traditional interpretation of "alienation," but we are here *in odiosis* and should not extend the law beyond what it strictly demands.[30]

The solemnities which must be observed vary according to the classification of goods made in Canons 534, 1 and 1532. Precious articles, made so by reason of notable worth, intrinsic or extrinsic, such as vessels, vestments, statuary, paintings, etc., can be alienated only by the express permission of the Holy See. The same authorization is required for the alienation of goods not held as precious,[31] whose value[32] exceeds thirty thousand francs or about six thousand dollars.[33] No permission other than this is required.[34] In religious communities the apostolic indult is likewise required for alienation of goods valued at more than six thousand dollars. In any of these cases if the person or persons alienating knowingly omit to obtain the permission of the Holy See they incur the excommunication.

The following regulations are laid down in the Code, though not under pain of censure, for the alienation of ecclesiastical goods of lesser value. Local Ordinaries are empowered to alienate or to contract to the extent of a thousand francs, or about two hundred dollars, but even

29 Cf. Chelodi, l. c., n. 79; Eichman, "Die Zenzuren," n. 54.

30 Can. 19 and 2219. 3.

31 These regulations do not apply to goods which, if not alienated, would anyhow be lost to the Church—"quae servando servari non possunt." Can. 1530, 1.

32 I. e., the estimate of value made in writing by trustworthy experts, not necessarily the amount received for the goods. Response of Pontif. Comm. Nov. 24, 1920.

33 At the present rate of exchange the amount would be equivalent to about twenty-two hundred dollars. However, the law is made to be permanent and supposes normal conditions.

34 The Third Plen. Council of Baltimore in this case required also the consent of the Diocesan Consultors, n. 20.

in this case they need the consent of those whose interests are affected by the transaction, and should, if the case be of importance, consult the Council of Administration.[35] When the value concerned is between one thousand and thirty thousand francs ($200 and $6,000) the Local Ordinary may again act without the special permission of the Holy See, but not unless he has obtained the consent of the Diocesan Consultors, the Council of Administration and those whose interests are affected. In religious communities goods of less value than six thousand dollars can be alienated upon the written permission of the Superior of the body, and the consent, secretly given, of its Chapter or Counsellors.[36] Religious women of diocesan jurisdiction, however, require the written consent of the Local Ordinary and also of the Regular Superior of the Order if their house is subject to such person.

Bishops can no longer be held exempt from the censure, as was contended by some authors under the old law.[37] For the Const. of Paul II, upon which the exemption was based, is no longer the norm of the censure, and besides they are not expressly exempted, but are implicitly included, in virtue of Can. 2347, 2.[38]

IV. Const. *Apost. Sedis:*

> "Negligentes sive culpabiliter omittentes denuntiare infra mensem confessarios, sive sacerdotes a quibus sollicitati fuerint ad turpia in quibuslibet casibus expressis a praedecessoribus Nostris Greg. XV, Const. "Universi" 10 Aug. 1611; et Bened. XIV, Const. "Sacramentum Poenitentiae" 1 Jun. 1741."

Codex I.C., Can. 2368, 2:

> "Fidelis . . . qui scienter omiserit eum, a quo sollicitatus fuerit, intra mensem denuntiare contra praescriptum can. 904, incurrit in excom-

35 A committee over which the Ordinary presides and which advises him in the administration of ecclesiastical property. Cf. Cann. 1520; 1532, 2; 1539, 2.

36 Cf. Can. 516.

37 Cf. D'Annibale, l. c., n. 177; Pennachi, II. p. 142; Genicot, l. c., n. 69; Wernz, III, n. 170.

38 Cf. Can. 2227, 2.

> municationem latae sententiae nemini reservatam, non absolvendus nisi postquam obligationi satisfecerit aut se satisfacturum serio promiserit."

In Chapter I, Art. XV, we discussed the censure of excommunication which has been newly instituted for the crime of false denunciation of a confessor.[39] Here we have to deal with the law itself which requires that denunciation be made.

When Pope Gregory XV extended to the Universal Church[40] the Const. *Cum sicut* of Pius IV, in which confessors guilty of solicitation *ad turpia* were ordered to be punished by the Inquisition,[41] he amplified that Constitution by introducing a rigorous mandate obliging those who were solicited to denounce the offending priest to the Inquisition or to a Local Ordinary and commanding confessors to apprise their penitents of this duty under pain of being punished as the soliciting priests themselves.[42]

Benedict XIV, confirming the Const. of Gregory XV, forbade the absolution of penitents who had been solicited, until they had effectively made the denunciation to the competent authority or at least had promised to do so as soon as they were able.[43] In the meantime, March 10, 1677, the Holy Office had decreed that all the faithful were bound to denounce confessors whom they know to be guilty of this offense, and excommunication reserved to the Holy See as long as they refused to denounce and thereafter to the Ordinary, was incurred by those who neglected this duty. But since Benedict XIV, in a later law, held only the penitents themselves, the former law was thereby partly abrogated.

Pius IX in the Const. *Apost. Sedis* confirmed the Const. of Benedict XIV, but abrogated the reservation of ab-

39 Cf. Can. 2363.

40 Const. *Universi* Aug. 30, 1622.

41 Apr. 16, 1561, to the Inquisitor General of Spain.

42 Cf. Decr. S. C. S. Off Sept. 24, 1665, prop. 6, 7, damn.; Denziger-Bannwart, 1106 ss.

43 Const. *Sacr. Poenit.* June 1, 1741.

solution from the censure. The denunciation was required to be made within a month (*tempus utile*) computed from the day the penitent learned of the obligation, the censure and the space of time allowed; and including only the time in which he was able, without grave inconvenience, to perform the denunciation to the Local Ordinary or to the Holy Office.[44]

The Code does not depart from the former legislation in this respect, and hence nothing more need be said here. It may be observed that solicited persons under the age of puberty, since they are now excused from all penalties *latae sententiae,* are not comprehended by Can. 2368, 2, although, by Can. 904, they are obliged to make the denunciation.

V. When Pius IX declared in the Const. *Apost. Sedis* that the censures of excommunication directly enacted by the Council of Trent should continue in force, he made an exception of the unreserved excommunication decreed in Session IV concerning the edition and use of Sacred Books. He declared that thenceforth only they should be subject to that censure

> "Qui libros de rebus sacris tractantes sine Ordinarii approbatione imprimunt aut imprimi faciunt." [45]

Codex I.C., Can. 2318, 2:

> "Auctores et editores qui sine debita licentia sacrarum Scripturarum libros vel earum adnotationem aut commentarios imprimi curant, incidunt ipso facto in excommunicationem nemini reservatam."

The Council of Trent[46] had decreed that the Sacred Scriptures be printed in the most correct manner possible, and that it was unlawful to print or cause to be printed

44 Wernz, l. c., III, n. 471.
45 Const. *Ap. Sed.*
46 Sess. IV, de Canonicis Scripturis.

any books whatsoever dealing with sacred matters, without the name of the author; nor was anyone permitted to sell such books in the future or even to keep them unless the books had first been examined and approved by the Ordinary. This law was binding under pain of the anathema and fine imposed in the Canon of the last Lateran Council.[47]

Pius IX, in the words quoted above, restricted the censure to printing and causing to be printed books "treating of sacred things," thus using the expression of the Council of Trent. Hence the doubt as to what books were meant was not resolved by the decree of Pius IX, but the Holy Office explicitly declared that the law was restricted to the Sacred Scriptures.[48] And thus in the Const. *Officiorum ac munerum* of Leo XIII, whereby the entire legislation concerning the prohibition and censorship of books was recast, the present censure was declared to be incurred by those "who, without the approbation of the Ordinary, print or cause to be printed the books of the Sacred Scriptures, or annotations or commentaries on the same." [49] The law is similarly stated in the new Code, but, as we have already stated,[50] those who print the books are no longer liable to the censure, but those only who cause the books to be printed, whether they be the authors or the editors, the censure being newly extended to include the authors. We must also note that the word "scienter" does not appear in Par. 2 of Can. 2318, as it does in Par. 1, which deals with books propounding apostasy, heresy and schism. Hence crass or supine ignorance will not excuse the author or editor from the excommunication.

The censure punishes the violation of the law contained in Can. 1385, which reads: "Nisi censura ecclesiastica praecesserit, ne edantur, etiam a laicis, libri sacrarum Scripturarum vel eorundem adnotationes et

47 Fifth Lat. Coun. under Leo X, May 4, 1515.

48 Dec. 22, 1880.

49 Const. cit. Jan. 25, 1897, n. 48.

50 Chap. I, Art. II.

commentarios." The necessary permission can be given by the proper Ordinary of the author of the book, by the Ordinary of the place where the book is printed or the Ordinary of the place where the book is published. However, if the permission has been denied by one of these it cannot be asked of another without acquainting the latter with the denial.[51] This condition, it would seem, affects the lawfulness, not the validity, of the permission, so that if the permission is obtained without mention of the denial the excommunication is not incurred.[52]

VI. The Council of Trent, after declaring the impossibility of valid marriage between an abductor and his victim as long as she remained in his power, decreed that even though she be liberated and then freely elect to marry him, yet,

> "Raptor ipse ac omnes illi consilium, auxilium et favorem praebentes sint ipso jure excommunicati . . ."[53]

The decree of Trent was based upon Can. 26 of the Council of Chalcedon, which contemplated only that abduction which was perpetrated for the purpose of contracting marriage. Again, in Chapter 6 of Sess. XXIV of the Council of Trent there is question only of the abduction which constituted a diriment impediment to marriage, which is limited to "raptus intuitu matrimonii."[54] Hence the censure here imposed was contracted not by every sin of abduction, but only by that which had for its ultimate end the marriage of the abductor to his victim.[55] Besides excommunication the abductor, by the Tridentine law, suffered also perpetual infamy of law and ineligibility to all ecclesiastical offices and dignities.

51 Can. 1385, 2.

52 Cf. Cerato, l. c., n. 63.

53 Sess. XXIV, cap. 6, de ref. Matr.

54 Lehmkuhl, II, n. 774; Wernz, IV, n. 288; cf. Can. 1074.

55 Lehmkuhl, ibid.; Wernz, VI, n. 406.

Today the abductor incurs only one penalty *ipso facto* —exclusion from the legitimate ecclesiastical acts,[56] although additional punishments may be inflicted upon him. (Can. 2353.) The censure of excommunication, therefore, which the Council of Trent enacted ceased with the promulgation of the Code. (Can. 6, 5.)

But while punishments for the crime of abduction have been considerably diminished, the law itself is made to extend further than that of Trent. The latter was restricted to men who abducted in order to contract marriage with the one abducted.[57] Can. 2353 expressly includes also abduction done for the sake of satisfying lust, although this action does not constitute the diriment impediment of *raptus*. Again, the law is extended to the abduction of a minor against the will of her parents or guardians, even though she herself consent to the abduction. This case also was generally excluded from the Tridentine law, as regarded both impediment and penalties.[58]

VII. Another censure by which the Fathers of Trent sought to protect and insure the freedom of choice in marriage contracts was the excommunication imposed upon those masters and lords who forced men or women by threats and penalties to marry, against their own will, persons chosen by these masters:

> "Praecepit Sancta Synodus omnibus, cujuscumque gradus, dignitatis et conditionis existant, sub anathematis poena, quam ipso facto incurrant, ne quovis modo directe vel indirecte subditos suos, vel quoscumque alios cogant, quominus libere matrimonia contrahant." [59]

This censure, as has been pointed out by many authors,[60] was imposed not upon kings and emperors (for

56 Recited *taxative* in Can. 2256.

57 Loc. cit.

58 Cf. Pennachi, II, p. 253.

59 Sess. XXIV, cap. 9, de Ref. Matr.

60 Cf. Lehmkuhl, II, 982; Pennachi, II, 260.

these were not considered as affected by censures unless expressly mentioned),[61] but upon those lords, masters and nobles who held a *quasi-mean* authority and were responsible for the rights of their subjects.

Conditions having greatly changed since the time of the Council of Trent, the case which the decree contemplates would hardly ever occur in modern times. Some authors suggest that the censure might be incurred, before the Code, by a civil magistrate who would force a man and woman to continue to live as husband and wife after their marriage had been declared null by competent ecclesiastical authority, but it is doubtful whether the conditions of the Tridentine law were thus verified. The law being inexpedient, it does not appear in the Code.

VIII. The Council of Trent, furthermore, instituted two censures of excommunication in reference to the entrance of women into monasteries:

> A. "Anathemati Sancta Synodus subjicit omnes et singulas personas, cujuscumque qualitatis, vel conditionis fuerint, tam clericos quam laicos saeculares vel regulares, atque etiam qualibet dignitate fulgentes, si quomodocumque coegerint aliquam virginem, vel viduam, aut aliam quamcumque mulierem invitam, praeterquam in casibus in jure expressis, ad ingrediendum monasterium, vel ad suscipiendum habitum cujuscumque religionis, vel ad emittendam professionem; quique consilium, auxilium, vel favorem dederint; quique scientes, eam non sponte ingredi monasterium, aut habitum suscipere, aut professionem emittere, quoque modo eidem actui vel praesentiam, vel consensum, vel auctoritatem interposuerint. . ."[62]

Codex I.C., Can. 2352:

> "Excommunicatione nemini reservata ipso facto plectuntur omnes, qualibet etiam dignitate fulgentes, qui quoquo modo cogant sive virum ad statum clericalem amplectendum, sive virum aut

61 Bonacina, "De Excom. in part." Disp. II, qu. II, pt. 6, n. 7.
62 Sess. XXV, cap. 18, de reg.

mulierem ad religionem ingrediendam vel ad emittendam religiosam professionem tam sollemnem quam simplicem, tam perpetuam quam temporariam."

Several important changes in the Tridentine law quoted above, it will be noted, are made in Can. 2352.

The spirit of this law is to safeguard the liberty of the individual and the peace that ought to reign in all religious houses. Hence it is that the law now forbids, under censure, the forcing of men as well as women, the former into the clerical state or into religion, the latter into religion, to which alone they are eligible. The clerical state is attained, and therefore the offence to which the censure is attached is completed, when the first tonsure is received.[63]

The Tridentine law dealt with entrance into a "monastery," which, by strict interpretation, was limited to that of an Order properly so-called.[64] Can. 2352 speaks of entrance into religion and therefore has a much wider extension, including as it does the entrance into the novitiate of any society, approved by legitimate ecclesiastical authority, whose members strive after evangelical perfection by observing the special laws of the society and by making public vows, either perpetual or temporary, the latter to be renewed when the time expires.[65]

Formerly the penalty could be incurred by forcing a woman to enter a monastery for no other purpose than to live apart from the world;[66] today she must actually enter the religious state, which she does only when admitted to a novitiate.[67] Postulants, as the word itself

63 Can. 108, 1. There are some who think the present law comprehends also the case of receiving minor or major Orders. Cf. Cerato, l. c., n. 66; Sole, n. 395. Contra: Chelodi, l. c., n. 81; Cavigioli, l. c., n. 178.

64 Pennachi, II, p. 274.

65 Can. 488, 1. Cf. Chelodi, l. c.; Cerato, l. c.

66 Sanchez, l. c., Lib. III, cap. 4; Lehmkuhl, l. c., p. 698.

67 Cf. Sole, l. c., n. 395. This is also implied in Can. 542, where the causes are recited which invalidate admission to the novitiate.

signifies, cannot be said to have entered religion, but rather seek admission thereto.

"Religious profession" in the Tridentine law, being strictly interpreted, was confined to the profession of solemn vows,[68] whereas Can. 2352 expressly comprehends every religious profession, whether the vows be solemn or simple, perpetual or temporary. Here, again, we notice the spirit of the law seeking to insure not only the freedom of the individual in choosing his or her state of life, but also the internal harmony of religious houses, which might be seriously disturbed by dissatisfied and restless members.

Co-operators in these crimes were formerly mentioned explicitly as liable to the censure. In the Code they are also included, provided their co-operation is that of principal accomplices, according to the tenor of Canons 2209 and 2231. "Coaction," which implies unwillingness on the part of the victim, must here be understood in a strict sense. Hence it may be accomplished by force or relatively grave fear, but not by persuasion, promises, gifts, deceit and the like, for when these means are used the person is, indeed, induced unjustly, but is not coerced.[69]

Finally, the former law made exception of the cases in which it was lawful to compel a woman to enter a monastery (not, however, to assume the religious habit nor to make religious profession). There were two such cases: (a) when a wife, whose husband had made religious profession, was in danger of incontinence in the world;[70] (b) when an adulterous wife, repudiated by her husband, was in danger of leading a vicious life.[71] These exceptions may now be considered abrogated, since they are not mentioned in connection with the censure nor in the Canons dealing with the profession of married persons and the rights of adulterous consorts.[72]

68 Pennachi, II, p. 274.

69 Cf. Lehmkuhl, l. c., n. 983; Téphany, l. c., n. 510 ss.; Sabetti-Barrett, "Compend. Theol. Moral." ed. 26a, n. 1015.

70 C. 18, X, de convers. conjug. III, 32.

71 C. 19, X, de convers. conjug., III, 32.

72 Cann. 1119-1132. Cf. Cerato, l. c.

B. In the same chapter of the *Canons and Decrees of the Council of Trent* we read:

> "Simili quoque anathemati subjicit eos, qui sanctam virginum, vel aliarum mulierum voluntatem, veli accipiendi, vel voti emittendi, quoquo modo sine justa causa impedierint."

This law was founded upon two ancient decrees. The Third Council of Toledo (589) excommunicated those who prevented widows or virgins from embracing a life of chastity;[73] the Council of Tribur (895) forbade any one to prohibit a young woman from "taking the veil" after she had attained the age of twelve years.[74]

The censure imposed by Trent was intended to protect the liberty of women in assuming the habit or, after being invested with the habit, making their solemn profession.[75] The law was particularly intended to eliminate the practice of parents who, to ameliorate their social and financial station by arranging favorable marriages, put obstacles in the way of their daughters who manifested the desire and will to enter the religious life.[76] Conditions have changed considerably since the days of Trent and the severe punishment is no longer required to insure the freedom in choosing one's station in life. Hence in the Code we find no reference to the Tridentine or ancient legislation in this matter.

IX. The Fathers of Trent obliged "secular magistrates," i. e., those who exercised secular and civil jurisdiction, to assist the bishops in restoring and preserving the cloister of nuns. The obligation was made to bind under pain of excommunication unreserved.[77]

73 C. 16, C. XXXII, q. 2.

74 C. 16, C. XXXII, q. 2.

75 The stricter interpretation followed by most commentators; in the time of the Council of Trent there were very few Congregations of simple vows.

76 Cf. Pennachi, II, 282 ss.

77 Sess. XXV, cap. 5, de reg.

In enacting this law the Council renewed the decree which Boniface VIII made when he declared the law of the cloister. The Tridentine decree, however, gradually fell into disuse, so that when the Constitution *Apostolicae Sedis* was promulgated, in 1869, authorities were divided as to the revival of the censure imposed by Trent.[78] Avanzini held that in the existing state of society the censure had, for want of use, fallen into desuetude.[79] The fact was rather, as Pennachi observes,[80] that, on account of the peculiar circumstances of the times, the law requiring the magistrates to look after the cloisters could not be enforced.[81] This, no doubt, accounts for the omission of the censure from the newly promulgated law.[82]

X. In addition to the foregoing censures, certain commentators[83] on the Const. *Apostolicae Sedis* cited three other unreserved censures of excommunication from the Council of Trent as being confirmed by Pius IX. These censures were pronounced: (a) upon those teaching, preaching or pertinaciously asserting that sacramental confession is not necessarily required of the person who is consciously in the state of mortal sin and has a "copia confessarii," before he approach the Sacrament of the Holy Eucharist;[84] (b) upon those who deny that clandestine marriages, entered into with the free consent of the parties, are true and ratified marriages as long as the Church does not render them null; and, (c) upon those who affirm that the marriages of children, contracted without the consent of their parents, are

78 Cf. Pennachi, II, p. 237; Varceno, "Compend. Theol. Moral.," T. II, p. 507.

79 "De Const. 'Apost. Sedis'" Rome, 1872, p. 121, note 35.

80 Loc. cit.

81 Cf. Vecchiotti, op. cit. II, p. 366.

82 Cf. Can. 2342.

83 Wernz, VI, pp. 464-465; Bargilliat, n. 1688; Pennachi, II, p. 243 ss.

84 Sess. XIII, cap. 7, Can. 2, de Euch. Cf. Can. 856.

invalid and that the parents may arbitrarily ratify them.[85]

These censures pertained rather to the field of dogma, and, besides, were comprehended in Art. I of the series of excommunications reserved *simpliciter* to the Holy See, where excommunication was inflicted upon those who teach or defend propositions condemned by the Holy See.[86] The censures, therefore, do not call for special discussion here.

XI. It remains now to consider one other non-reserved censure of excommunication which was in force prior to the Code of 1918.

Pope Urban VIII, Feb. 22, 1633, inflicted excommunication *latae sententiae* upon missionaries who engaged in commercial trading or business, personally or through others, directly or indirectly, for their own gain or that of their communities.[87] The censure affected all missionaries in the East Indies and the Jesuit provinces of China and Japan. Notwithstanding this severe penalty, the prohibition was still ignored and scandals continued to arise. Wherefore Pope Clement IX extended the law to the missionaries in North and South America, and obliged the respective Superiors, likewise under pain of excommunication, to remove offending missionaries from the place where they may have violated the law.[88]

This censure was not included by Pius IX, either directly or indirectly, in the exclusive list of censures *latae sententiae* published in 1869. Hence, it was rightly held as having been abrogated by that Constitution. However, the Holy Office, in 1872, brought the matter to the attention of the Supreme Pontiff, who directed the Congregation *de Propaganda Fide* to send a circular let-

85 Sess. XXIV, cap. 1, de ref.

86 Cf. Lehmkuhl, l. c., n. 980m ss.; Vecchiotti, III, p. 367; also Ch. II, Art. I.

87 Const. *Ex debito.*

88 Const. *Sollicitando,* June 17, 1669.

ter to all local Ordinaries, declaring the censure to retain its force.

In the common law of today we read: "Prohibeantur clerici per se vel per alios negotiationem aut mercaturam exercere sive in propriam sive in aliorum utilitatem." (Can. 142.) Religious are likewise bound by this law, according to Can. 592. The punishment of violators now rests with the judgment of the respective Ordinaries of the offenders. (Can. 2380.) The censure of excommunication is not renewed and must be considered abrogated in view of the sweeping declaration contained in Can. 6, 5.

CHAPTER V

Excommunications Concerning the Election of the Roman Pontiff and the Internal Government of Orders of Regulars, etc.

Towards the end of the Const. *Apostolicae Sedis* we read:

> "Quae vero censurae sive excommunicationis, sive suspensionis, sive interdicti, Nostris, aut Praedecessorum Nostrorum Constitutionibus, aut sacris canonibus praeter eas, quas recensuimus, latae sunt, atque hactenus in suo sigore perstiterunt sive pro Romani Pontificis electione, sive pro interno regimine quorumcumque ordinum et institutorum regularium, necnon quorumcumque collegiorum, congregationum, coetum locorumque piorum cujuscumque nominis aut generis sint, eas omnes firmas esse, et in suo robore permanere volumus et declaramus."

We have here, then, to consider two classes of excommunications which Pius IX confirmed in the words just quoted: (a) those incurred in connection with the election of the Roman Pontiff, and (b) those instituted in the interest of the internal government of Orders of Regulars and other pious institutes.[1]

A. Election of the Roman Pontiff.

The censures of excommunication which were incurred on account of offenses committed in connection with the election of the Roman Pontiff, and which were affected by the confirmatory clause of the Const. *Apost.*

1 The suspensions and interdicts confirmed in this pronouncement will be treated in Chapters VI and VII respectively.

Sedis, are found exclusively in the Const. *Aeterni Patris Filius*, published by Pope Gregory XV, November 13, 1621.[2] In this Constitution seven species of transgression were enumerated, to each of which was attached the penalty of excommunication *latae sententiae*. The absolution from these censures was reserved to the Roman Pontiff *specialissimo modo*, as we might say, since, except in danger of death, no one else—not even the "Major Poenitentiarius"—could absolve the delinquent.[3]

The several acts prohibited by Gregory XV under pain of excommunication may be summed up as follows:

1. Transgressing any of the rules laid down in the Constitution for voting and the several methods of voting in electing the Roman Pontiff. (Cit. Const. n. 14.)
2. Violating the secrecy imposed upon the person who fills in the ballot of a Cardinal unable to write. (n. 15.)
3. Violating the secrecy of the ballot of a sick Cardinal. (n. 16.)
4. Refusing to enter the Conclave when summoned for the purpose of election, or refusing to vote twice daily. (n. 17.)
5. Entering pacts or giving or soliciting promises for the election or the exclusion of a candidate. (n. 18.)
6. Electors, elected and co-operators participating in an election held outside the secret conclave or without having two-thirds of the votes of the Cardinals present. (n. 19.)
7. Changing any part of the Const. *Aeterni Patris Filius* or setting up anything contrary to its provisions. (n. 20.)

These, then, were the offenses for which excommunication might be incurred in papal elections after Oct. 12, 1869.

Pius X, cognizant of the inordinate number and the obscurity of the laws enacted through centuries for the

2 Cf. Const. *Decet Romanum Pontificem*, Mar. 12, 1622, Bullarium, Vol. XII, p. 619.

3 Cit. Const.

election of the Roman Pontiff, published, Dec. 25, 1904, the Const. *Vacante Sede Apostolica,* in which the former provisions were, as far as possible, confirmed, and by which papal elections were thenceforth to be governed. The elections are still regulated by this Constitution in virtue of Canons 160 and 2330.[4]

It must be noted that the censures and other penalties that were in force prior to December 25, 1904, were not abrogated by the Const. *Vacante Sed. Ap.*"[5] However, those of them that are not found in that Constitution, which is made part of the Code, are now abrogated by reason of their omission.[6]

The crimes that are punished with excommunication *latae sententiae* by the Const. *Vacante Sede Apost.* are as follows:

1. Cardinals, not impeded by ill health, failing to repair to the place of election when the customary signal has been given. (n. 37.)

2. Sending the daily papers or periodicals outside the Conclave. (n. 50.)

3. Violating the secrecy imposed upon Cardinals and all others assisting in the Conclave regarding all that pertains to the election or takes place within the Conclave. (n. 51.)

4. Cardinals violating the secrecy required regarding the voting and matters discussed in the Congregations of Cardinals either before or during the Conclave. (n. 52.)

5. Violating the secrecy imposed upon one who fills in a ballot in the name of a Cardinal unable to write. (n. 69.)

6. Simony in the election of the Roman Pontiff. (n. 79.)

4 Can. 160: "Romani Pontificis electio unice regitur const. Pii X *Vacante Sede Apostolica,* 25 Dec. 1904; ..." Can. 2330: "Quod attinet ad poenas statutas in delicta quae in eligendo Summo Pontifice committi possunt, unice standum const. Pii X *Vacante Sede Apostolica,* 25 Dec. 1904."

5 Cf. Wernz, II, n. 585.

6 Can. 6, 5.

7. Arranging, while the Roman Pontiff is still living, and without his consent, for the election of his successor; offering or soliciting votes for this purpose; or deliberating on the question in private meetings. (n. 80.)

8. Accepting from any civil power, under any pretense whatever, the mission of presenting the "veto" or "exclusiva," even in the form of a simple desire; or, whatever be the means through which the "veto" has come to one's knowledge, to make it known directly or indirectly, mediately or immediately, orally or in writing, either to the College of Cardinals or to Cardinals individually, before or during the Conclave. This prohibition extends to any intervention, intercession or any other attempt made by lay powers to interfere in the election of the Roman Pontiff. (n. 81.)[7]

9. Cardinals entering into pacts or agreements, or making promises, or binding themselves in any way, to give their votes to some person or persons. (n. 82.)

10. Impugning the letters, treating of any business whatsoever, which emanate from the Roman Pontiff before his coronation. (n. 88.) This is the only one of the group of censures that affects all the faithful; the others are incurred either by Cardinals only or by Cardinals and the other persons who assist in the Conclave.

The penalty incurred *ipso facto* by any of the abovenamed offenses is excommunication, and the absolution therefrom is reserved to the Supreme Pontiff in such a way that, except in danger of death, not even the Cardinal Major Poenitentiarius has power to absolve.[8] There is, then, a difference, as to the manner of reservation, between this class of censures and the four excommunications found in the Code as *very specially* reserved.[9] Nevertheless, since these ten censures are not excluded from the scope of the faculties afforded by Can. 2254,[10]

7 This is a confirmation of the law promulgated by Pope Pius X, Jan. 20, 1904, in the Const. *Commissum Nobis.*

8 Const. *Vacante Sed. Ap.*

9 Cann. 2320, 2343, 1, 2367 and 2369, 1; cf. Chap. I.

10 "Quoquo modo reservatis."

we may infer that they are, in this respect, assimilated to the other censures that are reserved *specialissimo modo*.[11]

B. Internal Government of Orders Regular and Other Pious Institutes.

Pius IX confirmed also those excommunications which had been enacted for the internal government of Orders and Institutes of Regulars and of Colleges, Congregations and other Pious Associations and Places, and which were in force at the time of the promulgation of the Const. *Apost. Sedis.* Since there is question here of the *internal* government only, it follows that only those censures are here concerned which promote the spiritual good of the respective bodies.[12] Of these four excommunications are found to have been in force when the Constitution was published:

1. The first was enacted by Pope Clement V in the Council of Vienne against monks who would presume to approach a secular tribunal in order to do harm to their own prelates or to their monasteries.[13]

2. In the same decree monks were forbidden, under pain of excommunication, to keep arms within the monastery walls without the permission of the abbot.[14]

3. The third is that contained in the Const. *Ubi Gratiae* of Gregory XIII[15] and the Const. *Decori* of Pius V,[16] imposed upon those Superiors of Regulars and of Monasteries, who violate, or permit to be violated, the law of the cloister. This censure has already been treated in this work. (See Chap. II, Art. VI and VII.)

4. The fourth was enacted by Paul V[17] against those Superiors of Regulars, who fail to denounce subjects who

11 Cf. Chelodi, l. c., n. 68; Capello, l. c., n. 184; contra, Cerato l. c., n. 107.

12 Cf. Pennachi, II, p. 543.

13 C. 1, de statu monach., III, 10, in Clem.

14 Ibid.

15 Feb. 1, 1570.

16 June 13, 1575.

17 Const. *Romanus Pontifex*, Sept. 1, 1606, n. 5.

are heretical or suspected of heresy. The censure was confirmed by Alexander VII.[18]

These punishments, the third excepted, since they are not mentioned in the Code of 1918, must now be considered abrogated.[19] The first mentioned may find application in Can. 2341, by which excommunication is incurred in certain cases of violation of the *privilegium fori*, although this latter censure differs specifically from the former and is reserved, whereas none of the four censures cited above were considered reserved.

18 Const. *Licet alias*, July 8, 1660.
19 Can. 6, 5.

CHAPTER VI

SUSPENSIONS

The Constitution *Apostolicae Sedis*, after declaring, explicitly or implicitly, the excommunications *latae sententiae* that were thenceforth to have the force of general laws, concerned itself with those censures which are peculiar to clerics, namely, suspensions. In the Fifth Series of the Constitution are enumerated seven suspensions *latae sententiae* reserved to the Roman Pontiff,[1] which will be treated in the present chapter. Besides these we shall consider the eight suspensions enacted *directly* by the Council of Trent (and confirmed, therefore, by Pius IX), the four suspensions that were enacted in various decrees after the publication of the aforesaid Constitution, but before that of the Code, and finally the seven suspension-censures newly established by the Code itself.

We shall treat first, and in their own numerical order, the suspensions specifically mentioned in the Constitution.

A. Suspensions reserved to the Roman Pontiff.

I. Const. *Apost. Sedis:*

> "Suspensionem ipso facto incurrunt a suorum beneficiorum perceptione ad beneplacitum S. Sedis capitula et conventus ecclesiarum et monasteriorum aliique omnes, qui ad illarum regimen et administrationem recipiunt episcopos aliosve praelatos de praedictis ecclesiis seu monasteriis apud

1 Although the Const. *Apost. Sedis* purported to deal with censures only, yet we shall find in this group six sentences of suspension which, since their absolution did not depend on the cessation of the culprit's contumacy, cannot be considered true censures, but rather vindictive penalties, according to the distinction made in the Code (Cann. 2241 and 2286) and even in the Constitution itself.

eandem S. Sedem quovis modo privisos, antequam ipsi exhibuerint Litteras Apostolicas de sua promotione."

Codex I.C., Can. 2394:

"Qui beneficium, officium vel dignitatem ecclesiasticum propria auctoritate occupaverit vel ad ea electus, praesentatus, nominatus in eorundem possessionem vel regimen seu administrationem sese ingesserit antequam necessarias litteras confirmationis vel institutionis acceperit easque illis ostenderit quibus de jure debet: . . .

3. Capitula vero, conventus aliique omnes ad quos spectat, hujusmodi electos, praesentatos vel nominatos ante litterarum exhibitionem admittentes, ipso facto a jure eligendi, nominandi vel praesentandi suspensi maneant ad beneplacitum Sedis Apostolicae."

This punishment had its origin in a decree of Pope Boniface VIII,[2] by which (a) Bishops, Abbots and other Prelates elected by the Holy See were prohibited, under pain of suspension, from assuming the administration of their respective offices, benefices and places without first having the Letters Apostolic in which their election was confirmed; and (b) Chapters and Convents of churches or monasteries were forbidden, under pain of suspension from the fruits of their benefices, to receive or to render obedience to such persons before the Letters Apostolic were exhibited by the incoming prelates. The former penalty was not included by Pius IX in the Const. *Apost. Sedis,* nor even in the Const. *Romanus Pontifex.*[3] For this latter Constitution, while it punishes persons who, having been nominated or presented for vacant churches, assume the administration thereof before presenting the necessary Letters, contemplates only those who are nominated or presented by lay powers.[4] We must not, then, confound the present case with that which is concerned

2 C. 1, de electione, I, 3, in extrav. comm.
3 Aug. 28, 1873.
4 Cf. Chap. I, Art. XIII.

in the Const. *Romanus Pontifex* and which will be discussed further on in the present chapter.[5]

Under the new discipline suspension is likewise incurred *ipso facto* by the Chapters, Convents and all others (Diocesan Consultors) whose business it is to examine and recognize the Letters presented by the prospective incumbent, if they admit the person before the Letters are shown. The nature of the suspension, however, is changed. Formerly the delinquents were suspended "a perceptione beneficiorum," or, according to the more common opinion, from receiving the fruits of those benefices which were possessed by them in common. The penalty is now suspension from the right of electing, nominating and presenting any person for a benefice, office or dignity of any kind[6] and is reserved, as formerly, to the Holy See. From the nature of this penalty it will be seen that only those persons are liable to the penalty who have a part in the conferring of the administration, as, e. g., the Diocesan Consultors, not those, for instance, who offer obedience to the person unlawfully received, or who render him an account of the status of the church or benefice assumed.[7]

II. Const. *Apost. Sedis:*

> "Suspensionem per triennium a collatione Ordinum ipso jure incurrunt aliquem ordinantes absque titulo Beneficii vel patrimonii cum pacto ut ordinatus non petat ab ipsis alimenta."

Codex I.C., Can. 2373:

> "In suspensionem per annum ab ordinum collatione Sedi Apostolicae reservatam ipso facto incurrunt:
>
> 3. Qui aliquem ad ordines majores sine titulo canonico promoverint contra praescriptum can. 974, 1, n. 7; . . ."

5 Art. XVI.
6 Cf. Can. 2279, 2, 7.
7 Cf. Chelodi, l. c., n. 105.

Pius IX, in the present article, renewed a decree of Gregory IX, which is found in the Decretals under the title "De Simonia" because this transaction bears at least the appearance of simony.[8] By that decree both the ordaining bishop and the subject ordained were suspended, the former from conferring orders for three years, the latter from exercising the order or orders thus received until he had been dispensed by the Holy See. However, Pius IX retained only the suspension which affected the ordaining prelate. The one ordained without a canonical title, or who, after ordination, lost his title, suffered no penalty *latae sententiae*, nor was he *per se* prohibited from exercising his orders.

The law of today is more extensive than that of Pius IX. Under the latter, in order that suspension be incurred, the bishop must not only promote to sacred orders one who lacked a title, whether of benefice or of patrimony, but this with the understanding that the ordained was not to seek sustenance from him. If either element were lacking the suspension was not contracted. Today the penalty is incurred by ordaining anyone, whether the subject of the ordaining bishop or not, who lacks a canonical title. For secular clerics this title is a benefice or, in the absence of this, a patrimony[9] or a pension.[10] In lieu of these the title "servitii dioecesis" is recognized as canonical and, in places that are under the jurisdiction of the S. Congr. de Propaganda Fide, the title of the "Mission," in such a way that the one thus ordained is bound by oath to devote himself perpetually to the service of the diocese or mission under the authority of the Local Ordinary.[11] For Regulars the canonical title is solemn religious profession, or the title of "Poverty"; for religious of simple perpetual vows, the title "Mensae Communis" or "Congregationis" or some other title which

8 C. 45, X, de Simonia, V, 3; cf. Pennachi, II, p. 355 ss.

9 The patrimony must be peacefully, i. e., truly possessed, without fraud and in due form of law. Cf. Capello, n. 171.

10 The title must be secure for the whole life of the person ordained, and sufficient for his decent sustenance. Can. 979.

11 Can. 981.

a particular Constitution may provide. For all other religious, since they governed by the law of seculars, the canonical title is that of the secular clerics.[12]

In the new penal law no mention is made of ordination with the understanding that the ordained shall not seek sustenance from the ordaining prelate. This agreement is by Can. 980, 3, declared to be void of any binding force, and it is further required that any one who, without apostolic indult, *knowingly* ordains, or permits to be ordained, a subject who lacks a canonical title, is bound, together with his successors, to provide for the necessary sustenance of that subject until it has otherwise been provided for.

Finally, the suspension, which formerly lasted for three years, is now restricted to the term of one year.

III. Const. *Apost. Sedis:*

> "Suspensionem per annum ab ordinum administratione ipso jure incurrunt ordinantes alienum subditum etiam sub praetextu beneficii statim conferendi, aut iam collati, sed minime sufficientis, absque ejus Episcopi litteris dimissorialibus, vel etiam subditum proprium, qui alibi tanto tempore moratus sit, ut canonicum impedimentum contrahere ibi potuerit, absque Ordinarii ejus loci litteris testimonialibus."

Codex I.C., Can. 2373:

> "In suspensionem per annum ab ordinum collatione Sedi Apostolicae reservatam ipsi facto incurrunt:
>
> 1. Qui contra praescriptum can. 955, alienum subditum sine Ordinarii proprii litteris dimissoriis ordinaverint;
>
> 2. Qui subditum proprium, qui alibi tanto tempore moratus sit ut canonicum impedimentum contrahere ibi potuerit, ordinaverint contra praescriptum can. 993, 4, 994."

The purpose of the present penalty is to protect the rights and authority of bishops from invasion by other

12 Can. 982.

bishops and to prevent the reception of Sacred Orders by unworthy persons. This is gathered from the Const. *Speculatores* of Innocent XII,[13] in which the law first appeared and regulations were laid down to govern bishops in the ordination of the subjects of other bishops.[14]

The article, as also Can. 2373, consists of two parts, the former dealing with the requirement of "dimissorial letters," in which is contained the written permission of the proper prelate of the subject that the subject may be ordained by a certain bishop other than his own;[15] the latter part is concerned with "testimonial letters," in which the good character and worthiness of the subject are attested.[16] In both cases the law applies to the conferring of all orders, even the first tonsure.[17]

It is important to notice the disparity between the old and the new law in the matter of determining the *Episcopus proprius* of the candidate for Orders. Formerly four titles were recognized: domicile, origin, benefice and familiar service. The latter two are no longer recognized; nor is mere origin or domicile a sufficient title *per se*. According to Can. 956, the bishop competent to ordain seculars is the one in whose diocese the ordinand (a) was born and has a domicile, or (b) has only a domicile and yet was not born there. In this latter case he must take an oath of his intention to remain permanently in that diocese.[18] This oath, however, is not required (a) when the ordinand has already been incardinated in the diocese by the reception of the first tonsure; or (b) when he is to be ordained "ad titulum servitii ecclesiae"; or (c) when he is a religious with simple perpetual vows.

With the exception of the changes just noted the law of Pius IX is confirmed in the new Code. Here we may

13 Nov. 4, 1694; cf. c. 2, de temp. ord. I, 9, in Sexto.

14 Cf. Conc. Trid. Sess. XXIV, c. 2, de ref.

15 Cf. Cann. 958, 964.

16 Cf. Cann. 993, 4; 994, 3.

17 Can. 950; the opposite view was formerly held in regard to the first tonsure. D'Annibale, l. c., n. 200; Reiffenst. I, XI, n. 170.

18 Cf. Const. *Speculatores*, X, n. 5.

again add that the suspension is not a censure, but a vindictive penalty, since it depends for cessation not upon the cessation of the contumacy of the delinquent bishop, but upon the will of the Holy See, to whom the penalty is reserved.

The second part of the article is not changed by the present law. Testimonial letters must (under pain of suspension for one year and reserved to the Holy See) be had from the ordinary of the place where the ordinand has dwelt for a time sufficient for contracting a canonical impediment. (Can. 993, 4.) This time is regularly six months after reaching the age of puberty, or fourteen years complete. (Can. 994, 1.) Formerly it was held that this period of time was sufficient if spent after the age of seven years has been attained, because from this time on one was capable of incurring censures and irregularities as canonical impediments.[19] For one who is engaged in military service a stay of three months in a diocese is sufficient time for incurring the impediment,[20] which was already decreed by the Congr. of the Council Sept. 19, 1893, and Jan. 26, 1895.

Even though one has already obtained testimonial letters from a local Ordinary for the above reason, yet if he has again spent the prescribed time in that diocese new letters are required to cover the latter period.

IV. Const. *Apost. Sedis:*

> "Suspensionem per annum a collatione ordinum ipso jure incurrit, qui, excepto casu legitimi privilegii, Ordinem sacrum contulerit absque titulo beneficii vel patrimonii clerico in aliqua Congregatione viventi, in qua sollemnis professio non emittitur, vel etiam religioso nondum professo."

The Council of Trent, which decreed that no secular should be ordained without the title of benefice or patrimony,[21] made no provision in this regard for Religious.

19 Cf. D'Annibale l. c., p. 128; Genicot, II, n. 439; Gasparri, "De Sacr. Ord." n. 731.

20 Can. 994, 1.

21 Sess. XXI, c. 2, de ref.

Hence it happened that clerics, living in common after the manner of regulars, and making only simple profession or no profession at all, left or were dismissed from the cloister and were ordained by certain bishops under the pretext of religion, and then, not having sufficient means of sustenance, resorted to ignoble begging or worse means of support.[22] For this reason Pope Pius V extended the Tridentine law to all male religious who lived in Congregations of simple vows or who, before they were solemnly professed, left the cloister. He, furthermore, declared that bishops who ordained such persons without the title of benefice or patrimony were *ipso facto* suspended for one year from conferring whatever orders they had thus unlawfully conferred. Pius IX, in confirming the decree of Pius V, made no distinction, but declared the offending bishops suspended simply "from the conferring of orders."

We have already seen from Can. 982 that the canonical title of regulars is solemn religious profession, or the title of Poverty. This is, therefore, the only way in which regulars, as such, may be promoted to sacred orders, in default of which they must have one of the other canonical titles in order to be ordained at all. Likewise, we have already stated that the religious of simple vows need, as canonical, the title "Mensae Communis" or "Congregationis" or some other title that may be provided for in their respective Constitutions.[23] The law, therefore, which is contained in the present article of the Const. *Apost. Sedis* is confirmed by the Code, which, in Can. 2373, 2, provides that suspension for one year from conferring orders is incurred *ipso facto* by promoting to major orders a candidate who lacks a canonical title.

V. Const. *Apost. Sedis:*

"Suspensionem perpetuam ab exercitio Or-

22 Cf. Pennachi, II, p. 385.
23 Chap. V, Art. II.

dinum ipso jure incurrunt Religiosi ejecti, extra religionem degentes."

Codex I.C., Can. 671.

"Si vero (religiosus votorum perpetuorum in sacris) dimittatur ob delicta minora iis de quibus in can. 670: (seu apostasia publica, fuga cum muliere, attentatione matrimonii, et iis quae infamia juris vel depositione vel degradatione puniuntur)

1. Ipso facto suspensus manet, donec a Sancta Sede absolutionem obtinuerit; . . ."

The S. Congregation of the Council, at the instance of Pope Urban VIII, decreed[24] that dismissed religious who remained outside a religious house were *ipso facto* suspended perpetually from the exercise of their orders, and denied to Ordinaries the power to relax or moderate the suspension. Article V of the Constitution is a confirmation of that law. By a decree of the S. Congr. of Bishops and Regulars this penalty was extended to all, whether of temporal or perpetual vows, who were expelled or dismissed, whether they dwelt outside or not,[25] and was declared to embrace those also who had taken only simple vows. These had been considered exempt from the law by many authors.[26]

By the Code the penalty is likewise inflicted upon dismissed religious, though not upon all of these, as will be explained. Wherefore, the termination of the suspension has been placed upon a different basis. Formerly the suspension lasted as long as the dismissed religious remained outside. Upon his return or his entering the house of another religion the punishment ceased. Now, however, since his remaining outside the religion has no direct bearing upon the suspension, he remains suspended until he has received absolution from the censure. This absolution is simply reserved to the Holy See, and therefore can be granted, if the case be occult, by the Ordinary, personally or through his delegate, in virtue of Can. 2237, 2.

24 Sept. 21, 1624, n. 10

25 *Auctoris admodum*, Nov. 4, 1892.

26 Cf. Pennachi, II, p. 401; D'Annibale, l. c., n. 203; Sabetti-Barrett, l. c., n. 1021.

Can. 671 states that the present suspension is imposed upon those who have been dismissed for lesser offences than those mentioned in Can. 670. In the latter canon it is provided that religious in sacred orders who have publicly apostatized from the Catholic faith, fled with a woman or attempted even civil marriage (in which three cases they are *ipso facto* legitimately dismissed from religion)[27] and also those who have been dismissed for a crime which is, by the common law, punished with infamy of law,[28] deposition,[29] or degradation,[30] are perpetually forbidden to wear the ecclesiastical garb. In these cases the suspension would be superfluous, since such delinquents, in virtue of the penalties named, suffer the privation that this censure entails; and besides, the crimes above mentioned are punished with vindictive penalties, whereas the suspension here concerned is rather medicinal.[31].

VI. Const. *Apost. Sedis:*

> "Suspensionem ab ordine suscepto ipso jure incurrunt, qui eundem ordinem recipere praesumpserunt ab excommunicato vel suspenso, vel interdicto nominatim denuntiatis, aut ab haeretico vel schismatico notorio; eum vero, qui bona fide a quopiam eorum est ordinatus, exercitium non habere ordinis sic suscepti, donec dispensetur, declaramus."

Codex I.C., Can. 2372:

> "Suspensionem a divinis, Sedi Apostolicae reservatam, ipso facto contrahunt, qui recipere ordines praesumunt ab excommunicato vel suspenso vel interdicto post sententiam declaratoriam vel condemnatoriam, aut a notorio apostata, haeretico, schismatico; qui vero bona fide a quopiam eorum sit ordinatus, exercitio careat ordinis sic recepti donec dispensetur."

27 Can. 646.

28 Canons 2320, 2343, 2351, 2, 2356, 2357, 1.

29 Canons 2314, 1,2, 2320, 2322, 2328, 2350, 2354, 2, 2359, 2, 2379, 2394, 2, and 2401.

30 Canons 2314, 1, 3, 2341, 3, 3, 2354, 2, 2368, 1, and 2388, 1.

31 Cf. Cerato, l. c., n. 128; Cavigioli, l. c., n. 192.

In this article Pius IX confirmed substantially the ancient law on the reception of orders from excommunicated, suspended and interdicted bishops as well as notorious heretics and schismatics.[32] He restricted the law, however, to the exclusion of ordinations at the hands of simoniacal, irregular, deposed and degraded bishops. On the other hand, he no longer required that the excommunicated bishop in the case be *vitandus*.[33]

The penalty here concerned is a true censure. It is imposed for violation of the laws by which Catholics are forbidden to communicate in divine service with certain persons,[34] and is calculated to prevent the great disorders that would follow upon the illicit reception of orders from those persons.

The principal change effected by the new law is an increase in the severity of the penalty. The suspension which heretofore affected only the order or orders received in the forbidden ordination is now "suspensio a divinis" and prohibits, therefore, all exercise of the power of whatever orders one has received, whether this power has come with ordination or through privilege.[35]

"Apostates" are now specifically mentioned in the law; for if it be unlawful to receive Orders from heretics, who reject only a part of the Catholic belief, a fortiori one may not be ordained by an apostate, who has withdrawn himself completely from the faith.[36]

The suspension is incurred by one who receives orders in this illicit manner with full knowledge and deliberation. In other cases, i. e., when one receives orders in good faith from such persons, he incurs not a censure, for there can be no punishment where there has been no guilt, (Can. 2218, 2) but a privation, whereby he must abstain from exercising the orders unlawfully received until he has

32 C. 73, 111, C. 1, q. 1; C. 1, c. 1, q. 7; C. 5, c. IX, q. 1; C. 2, X, de ordinatis, etc., I, 13; C. 2, X, de schismaticis, V, 8.

33 Cf. Pennachi, II, 404 ss.

34 Cf. Cann. 2261, 3, 2275, 2, 2284, 1258.

35 Can. 2279, 2, 2.

36 Can. 1325, 2.

been dispensed, which may be done by his own Ordinary, since there is no indication of reservation in this regard.[37]

VII. Const. *Apost. Sedis:*

> "Clerici saeculares exteri ultra quattuor menses in Urbe commorantes ordinati ab alio quam ab ipso suo Ordinario absque licentia Cardinalis Urbis Vicarii, vel absque praevio examine coram eodem peracto, vel etiam a proprio Ordinario posteaquam in praedicto examine rejecti fuerint; necnon clerici pertinentes ad aliquem e sex episcopatibus suburbicariis, si ordinentur extra suam dioecesim, dimissorialibus sui Ordinarii ad alium directis quam ad Card. Urbis Vicarium; vel non praemissis ante ordinem sacrum suscipiendum exercitiis spiritualibus per decem dies in domo urbana Sacerdotum a Missione nuncupatorum, suspensionem ab ordinibus sic susceptis ad beneplacitum S. Sedis ipso jure incurrunt; episcopi vero ordinantes ab usu Pontificalium per annum."

Two classes of ordinands were affected by this law: clerics belonging to the six suburban dioceses of Rome and those of other dioceses outside Rome. Two penalties were contained herein. Clerics were suspended from the exercise of the orders illicitly received, and bishops ordaining contrary to the above prescriptions suffered suspension for one year from the exercise of the Pontifical acts.[38]

The article is a confirmation of laws which it was found necessary to enact in order to preserve the proper discipline in Rome, where so many candidates are presented for sacred orders.[39] At the present time there is no need of this specific legislation, the conferring of orders being sufficiently safeguarded by the general laws contained in the Code.[40] Hence no reference is made in the Code to the present article of the Constitution of Pius IX.

37 Cf. Gasparri, "De Sacr. Ord." II, n. 784.

38 Cf. Can. 337, 2.

39 Edict of the Card. Vicar under Clem. VIII, Nov, 24, 1603; decree of S. C. C. Sept. 21, 1624, under Urban VIII: edict of Card. Vicar under Bened. XIV, Mar. 20, 1743.

40 Lib. III, Tit. V.

B. Suspensions Enacted by the Council of Trent.

The following confirmation of Tridentine suspensions is found in the Constitution *Apostolicae Sedis:*

> "Denique quoscumque alios Sacrosanctum Concilium Tridentinum suspensos (aut interdictos) ipso jure esse decrevit, Nos pari modo suspensioni (vel interdicto) eosdem obnoxios esse volumus et declaramus."

We must, therefore, add to those already treated the suspensions that were directly enacted by the Fathers of the Council of Trent. Of these suspensions we find eight, which will here be cited and discussed in the light of the Code of 1918.

VIII. Conc. Trid. Sess. VI., cap. 5, de ref.:

> "Nulli episcopo liceat cujusvis privilegii praetextu pontificalia in alterius dioecesi exercere, nisi de Ordinarii loci expressa licentia, et in personas eidem Ordinario subjectas tantum. Si secus factum fuerit, episcopus ab exercitio pontificalium, et sic ordinati ab executione Ordinum sint ipso jure suspensi."

While the prohibition herein contained, since its purpose is to protect the authority and jurisdiction of residential bishops, is renewed in the new law, the penalties are no longer incurred by the violation of the law. The Council of Trent required that a bishop have the express permission of the bishop in whose diocese he wished to exercise the pontificals.[41] Today, although the law stipulates express permission, it is sufficient if the permission of the Local Ordinary can be reasonably presumed. (Can. 337, 1.) For the conferring of orders, however, the law does not allow a bishop to act on this presumption. Canon 1008 provides that "beyond his own territory a bishop cannot, without the permission of the Local Ordinary, confer orders whose conferring requires the use of the

41 I. e., to perform those sacred functions which, by liturgical law, require the pontifical insignia, or the mitre and the crozier. Can. 337, 2.

pontificals." This also confirms the opinion of those who held that without the aforesaid license a bishop could not ordain even his own subjects in the diocese of another.[42] Of course, if a bishop, whether at home or abroad, ordains the subject of another without the latter's permission, or dimissorials, the ordaining bishop is *ipso facto* suspended from the conferring of orders for the period of one year, and the one ordained is suspended from the order or orders thus received, as has already been noted.[43]

IX. Conc. Trid. Sees. VII, cap. 10, de ref.:

> "Non liceat Capitulis Ecclesiarum sede vacante, infra annum a die vacationis, ordinandi licentiam, aut litteras dimissorias seu reverendas, ut aliqui vocant, tam ex juris communis dispositione, quam etiam cujusvis privilegii aut consuetudinis vigore, alicui, qui beneficii ecclesiastici recepti sive recipiendi occasione arctatus non fuerit, concedere. Si secus fiat, . . . in majoribus (Constituti) ab executione ordinum ad beneplacitum futuri Praelati sint ipso jure suspensi."

The Code allows the Vicar Capitular (in this country the Administrator) more occasions than the Council of Trent afforded for granting dimissorial letters during the first year of a see's vacancy, since it adds to the exclusive reasons acknowledged by Trent that of providing for some certain need of the diocese, which brooks no delay. (Can. 958, 1, 3.) Such cases may now arise more frequently in places where, as a result of the late war, there exists a great want of priests or chaplains.[44] In that event the Vicar Capitular, or Administrator, may, with the consent of the Chapter or Diocesan Consultors,[45] grant dimissorials for the ordination of the number certainly required, or, if he has the necessary power, con-

42 Cf. Pennachi, II, p. 437 ss.

43 Cf. Cann. 2373, 2374.

44 France, for instance, was, even before the war, reported to be in need of about 3,000 priests. Cf. Augustine, "A Commentary on Canon Law," Vol. IV, Can. 958.

45 This consent was not required heretofore.

fer the orders himself.[46] For causes other than those mentioned the dimissorial letters given within the first year of the vacancy of a see by the Vicar Capitular or the Administrator are false. They are false also if given by others not authorized to do so,[47] if they are entirely forged, or if, being authentic, they have been substantially changed.[48]

With such false letters, or with no dimissorial letters at all, if one maliciously, i. e., in bad faith and with grave culpability, receives any order or orders he is *ipso facto* suspended from the exercise of those orders. (Can. 2374.) The Vicar Capitular, or Administrator, if he grant dimissorial letters otherwise than is provided in Can. 958, 1, 3, is *ipso facto* suspended *a divinis*. The penalty under the Tridentine law was suspension from office and benefice for one year.[49] We see, therefore, the wider extension of the new penal law in this matter, which comprehends not only the use of the false letters mentioned in the Tridentine decree, but that of any false dimissorial letters or no letters whatsoever.

Dispensation from the Tridentine suspension incurred by the subject of ordination was reserved to the incoming Ordinary of the vacant see. Canon 2374 is of wider extent and comprehends cases which occur *sede plena*. The present punishment is a true censure, depending for its cessation not upon any lapse of time or upon the will of the superior, but upon the delinquent's receding from his contumacy. (Can. 2242.)

Finally, the new law affects the reception of all orders, whereas formerly the penalty was incurred only in the reception of major orders, as we have seen. However, in the present law the first tonsure must be excepted, since it confers no powers from which one could be suspended.[50]

46 Can. 959, 969.
47 Cf. Can. 958, 964.
48 Cf. Capello, l. c., n. 179.
49 Cf. Can. 2409; Conc. Trid. Sess. 7, c. 10; Sess. 23, c. 10, de ref.
50 Cf. Can. 950; S. Alphons. VI, n. 788.

X. Conc. Trid. Sess. XIV, cap. 2, de ref.:

> "Nemo episcoporum, qui titulares vocantur, etiam si in loco nullius dioecesis, etiam exempto, aut aliquo monasterio cujusvis ordinis resederint, aut moram traxerint, vigore cujusvis privilegii sibi de promovendo quoscumque ad se venientes pro tempore concessi, alterius subditum, etiam praetextu familiaritatis continuae commensalitatis suae, absque sui proprii praelati expresso consensu aut litteris dimissoriis, ad aliquos sacros aut minores ordines vel primam tonsuram promovere seu ordinare valeat. Contra faciens ab exercitio pontificalium per annum, taliter vero promotus ab executione ordinum sic susceptorum, donec suo praelato visum fuerit, ipso jure sint suspensi."

This Tridentine penalty, which, like many other suspensions contained in the Const. *Apost. Sedis,* is rather of the nature of a "vindictive" punishment, is not expressly renewed in the Code. Nevertheless, the prohibition herein contained is doubtless in force and this under pain of reserved suspension for one year from conferring orders. For we read in Can. 2373: "In suspensionem per annum ab ordinum collatione Sedi Apostolicae reservatam ipso facto incurrunt: 1. Qui, contra praescriptum can. 955, alienum subditum sine Ordinarii proprii litteris dimissoriis ordinaverint; . . ." This certainly applies to titular bishops and even, as in the Tridentine law, to the conferring of the first tonsure.[51]

A candidate thus promoted to minor or major orders in bad faith falls under the censure of suspension which was treated in the previous article.

XI. Conc. Trid. Sess. XXIII, cap. 8, de ref.:

> "Unusquisque autem a proprio episcopo ordinetur. Quod si quis ab alio promoveri petat, nullatenus id ei, etiam cujusvis generalis aut specialis rescripti vel privilegii praetextu, etiam statutis temporibus permittatur, nisi ejus probitas ac mores, Ordinarii sui testimonio commendentur. Si secus

51 Cf. Capello, l. c., n. 169; Chelodi, l. c., n. 94.

> fiat, ordinans a collatione ordinum per annum et ordinatus a susceptorum ordinum executione, quamdiu proprio Ordinario videbitur expedire, sit suspensus."

In Art. III of the present chapter we considered the suspension incurred by bishops who ordain their own subjects without first having obtained testimonial letters from Ordinaries in whose dioceses the candidates may have dwelt long enough to contract a canonical impediment. Here, too, we are concerned with ordinations performed without testimonial letters, but only as regards the ordination of externs. Testimonial letters, as has already been stated, are letters which afford authentic testimony of the probity, character, freedom and worthiness of a candidate for orders.[52]

The abuse condemned in the present Tridentine decree is the ordination of another bishop's subject who, although he may have a special rescript or privilege to be thus ordained, yet has not presented testimonial letters from his own Ordinary. Here, again, it is evident that the purpose of the decree was to prevent unworthy candidates from receiving orders.[53]

The suspension, either of the ordaining prelate or the recipient of the orders does not appear in the new Code. Dimissorial letters are, of course, required under pain of suspension for both parties,[54] and these letters always contain the testimonials to which the decree of Trent refers.[55] The safeguard, therefore, is maintained.

To be ordained fraudulently without having the required testimonials, such as may be due from the Local Ordinary of a diocese in which one has spent six months, or three in the case of those engaged in military service, after reaching the age of puberty, is punishable today as one's bishop may deem proper, after considering the

52 Wernz, II, n. 29; Pennachi, II, p. 374 ss.

53 Cf. Penn. II, p. 370.

54 Can. 2373, 1 and 2374.

55 Wernz, II, n. 29, 2; Can. 960, 1.

circumstances in each case (Can. 2374); but no penalty is held out for the ordaining prelate, even though he be aware of the lack of the required testimonial letters. The same rule obtains in the promotion of ordinands who labor under a censure, an irregularity or some other canonical impediment to the reception of Orders.[56]

XII. Conc. Trid. Sess. XXIII, cap. 10, de ref.:

> Abbates, Collegia, Capitula, et alii quicumque quantumvis exempti, dimissorias litteras sibi non subditis concedentes, ab officio et beneficii per annum sint ipso jure suspensi.

By the decree above cited abbots were prohibited from infringing upon the rights of residential bishops in conferring tonsure and orders upon or granting dimissorial letters to those who had not become their subjects by solemn religious profession. However, in 1860, the Sacred Congregation of Religious declared that abbots might confer tonsure and minor orders, and hence grant dimissorial letters to those who were their subjects and who had taken only simple vows. This power is confirmed in the Code.[57] Colleges and Chapters, even of Cathedral churches, were forbidden by Trent to grant dimissorial letters to seculars not their subjects.[58]

The regulations laid down in the Code[59] to govern the granting of dimissorial letters confirm the Tridentine prohibition. The penalties are no longer found. Major Religious Superiors (abbots excepted as for tonsure and minor orders, as noted above) are obliged to send their ordinands, by dimissorial letters, to be ordained by the respective bishops in whose dioceses the religious houses to which the ordinands belong are situated.[60] With certain exceptions, this rule must always be adhered to, un-

56 Ibid.
57 Can. 964, 1, 2.
58 Decr. cit.
59 Can. 958-967.
60 Can. 965-967.

der pain of suspension of the Religious Superior for one month from the celebration of Mass.[61]

XIII. Conc. Trid. Sess. XXV, cap. 14, de ref.:

> **"Episcopi quoque, quod absit, si ab hujusmodi crimine (concubinatus) non abstinuerint, et a synodo provinciali admoniti, se non emendaverint, ipso facto sint suspensi."**

In the said Chapter 14 the Fathers of Trent prescribed the manner of dealing with clerics guilty of the crime of concubinage, so detestable in itself and so foreign to the clerical state; and, in the case of delinquent bishops, in whom the crime is even more reprehensible because of their high dignity and their duty of vigilance over others, decreed the sentence of suspension, as quoted above.[62]

The censure is not found in the new law. The case is rather committed to the judgment of the Roman Pontiff, in virtue of Can. 274, 4, whereby the Metropolitan is commissioned to see that the ecclesiastical discipline is strictly observed in the dioceses of his suffragans, and to report abuses to the Supreme Pontiff, who will determine any punishments that are to be inflicted.[63]

XIV. In the *Acts and Decrees of the Council of Trent* we read: "Cum promotis per saltum, si non ministraverint, episcopus ex legitima causa possit dispensare." [64] This suspension, since it was not directly enacted by the Council of Trent, but was the renewal of a formal law,[65] was not confirmed by the Const. *Apost. Sedis.*[66] The censure, therefore, which we shall cite below from the Code, may be considered new, although the prohibition remained in force after the Constitution of 1869.

61 Can. 2410.
62 Cf. c. 1, D. 34; c. 22, D. 81.
63 Cf. Can. 1557, 2, 1.
64 Sess. XXIII, cap. 14, de ref.
65 C. 1, D. 52.
66 Cf. D'Annibale, l. c., n. 225.

For the lawful [67] reception of an order the prior reception of the inferior orders is necessary,[68] and Can. 977 expressly forbids ordination *per saltum.* The penalty for the violation of this law is contained in Can. 2374. The ordaining prelate suffers no punishment, *latae sententiae* at least, but the candidate who maliciously advances to an order without having received the preliminary orders is *ipso facto* suspended from the Order or Orders thus illicitly received. It is evident that presumption on the part of the candidate is required.

XV. Another censure which was, by its omission, abrogated by Pius IX and is now restored is that incurred by one who, although lacking the required age, maliciously obtains ordination.[69]

Pius II, in 1461, decreed that those who, in bad faith, had themselves promoted to sacred orders were *ipso facto* suspended from the exercise of orders.[70] Bishops who conferred the first tonsure upon children under seven years of age were *ipso facto* suspended from conferring the tonsure.[71] Suspension (*ferendae sententiae*) from the conferring of all orders was incurred by the bishop who conferred major orders on one under the required age.[72]

The minimum age required in candidates for the respective major orders is, unless dispensation has been obtained from the Holy See, twenty-one years complete for sub-diaconate, twenty-two years complete for diaconate and twenty-four years complete for priesthood. (Can. 975.) No age is specified for the reception of the first tonsure and minor orders, but the candidate for tonsure must have at least begun his course in theology. (Can. 976, 1.) The penalty, incurred *ipso facto* by one

67 The validity of orders received *per saltum* cannot, for this reason, be doubted. Cf. S. C. S. Off. Mar. 21, 1842.

68 Can. 974, 1, 5.

69 Can. 2374.

70 Const. Cum ex sacrorum, Nov. 17, 1461.

71 C. 4, de Tempore etc., I, 9, in Sexto.

72 C. 14, X, I, 11.

who, in bad faith, receives Major Orders[73] while under the canonical age and having no dispensation, is suspension from the exercise of the order thus unlawfully received. The censure is not reserved.[74]

C. Suspensions Enacted After the Const. "Apostolicae Sedis"

After the publication of the Const. *Apost. Sedis*, but before the appearance of the new Code, four suspensions *latae sententiae* were introduced into the common law by various Constitutions and decrees. In order to demonstrate more completely the changes effected by the new law in suspensions of this nature, we shall here undertake a discussion of these censures, treating them in the chronological order of their enactment.

XVI. Const. *Romanus Pontifex*, Aug. 28, 1873:

> "Si vero aliqui ex praedictis (i. e., dignitates, etc., qui concedere et transferre in nominatum et praesentatum ad ecclesiam ejus curam, regimen et administrationem ante litteras Apostolicas exhibitas ausi fuerint) Episcopali charactere sint insigniti, in poenam suspensionis ab exercitio Pontificalium . . . ipso facto, absque ulla declaratione incidunt, S. Sedi pariter reservatam."

In Chapter I[75] we saw that, in virtue of this Constitution, excommunication reserved specially to the Holy See was incurred by certain classes of persons in the event that the dignitaries and Canons of Cathedral churches, without having been presented with the required Apostolic Letters, conceded and transferred the administration of their church to any person named or presented by a lay power. We saw, further, that that censure is no longer in force. In the same Constitution it was provided that if any of the offending dignitaries or

73 This penal law seems not to apply to the reception of tonsure or minor orders, since for their reception no age is specified.

74 Can. 2374.

75 Art. XIII.

Canons, or even the nominee himself, were a bishop, he incurred *ipso facto* suspension from the exercise of the Pontificals (and interdict *ab ingressu ecclesiae,* as will be seen in the following chapter) specially reserved to the Holy See.[76]

The suspension (and the interdict as well) imposed by the Const. *Romanus Pontifex* is not found in the Code. No special mention of bishops is made in Can. 2394, which now constitutes the law in the present matter, as has already been stated.[77] The suspension now obtaining affects only the right of election, nomination and presentation, and is incurred only by those who admit and not by the person admitted, although he becomes *ipso jure* incapable of holding the office and is otherwise punishable. The penalty, which was formerly a censure, is now "vindictive," being imposed "ad beneplacitum Sedis Apostolicae."

XVII. Decree of S. C. Conc. *Vigilanti studio,* concerning the collection of Mass stipends, May 25, 1893:

> "Si quis ex sacerdotali ordine contra enunciata decreta deliquerit, suspensioni a divinis, S. Sedi reservatae et ipso facto incurrendae, obnoxius sit; clericus autem sacerdotio nondum initiatus eidem suspensioni quoad susceptos Ordines similiter subjaceat, et inhabilis praeterea fiat ad superiores Ordines recipiendos. . . ."

In Art. IV of Chapter III we indicated the causes which led to the publication of the Decree *Vigilanti studio,* and considered the excommunication incurred by laics who engaged in the nefarious traffic in Mass stipends. Here we are concerned with the censure of suspension *a divinis* which, by the same decree, was inflicted *ipso facto* upon priests, and suspension *ab ordine* upon clerics not yet promoted to priesthood.

This penal law, as we have said, took its rise from a particular abuse of the times[78] and, as is the case with

76 Cf. Pennachi, II, p. 431.
77 Chap. VI, Art. I.
78 Decr. cit.

many such laws, is omitted from the Code. The abuse which the penalties were intended to correct are no less severely condemned today, and the penalties, too, are retained, but only in the form of *ferendae sententiae* punishments, which the Ordinary, in his judgment, may inflict. (Can. 2324.)

XVIII. Const. *Orientalium dignitas*, Nov. 30, 1894:

> "Missionarius quilibet latinus, e clero saeculari vel regulari, qui orientalem quempiam ad latinum ritum consilio auxiliove inducat, praeter suspensionem a divinis, quam ipso facto incurret; . . ."

The purpose of the Apostolic See in sending priests of the Latin rite into the territory of the Eastern Church is to afford assistance to the Patriarchs and Bishops of the respective places in the care of souls.[79] The Apostolic See, therefore, has always been careful to prevent any infringement upon the jurisdiction of these prelates or any diminution of the number of their subjects, which might result from missionaries' abuse of the faculties entrusted to them in the interest of the Eastern Church.[80] It was thus to safeguard the integrity of the Eastern Church that the present censure was instituted by Pope Leo XIII. The suspension could be incurred only by missionary priests of the Latin rite, whether secular or religious.

Since the censure is in no wise mentioned in the new Code it must be considered as abrogated.[81] This, of course, does not affect the prohibition to induce Orientals to adopt the Latin rite, but the Legislator has not seen fit to confirm, at this time, the suspension imposed by Leo XIII.

XIX. Decr. S. C. Conc., Jul. 12, 1900:

> "Clericus ut intestinis bellis et publicis contentionibus opem utcumque ferat, proprium residentiae locum absque justa causa, quae a legitima

79 Const. cit.

80 Const. *Demandatum* Bened. XIV, Dec. 24, 1743, n. 13.

81 Can. 6, 5.

> **ecclesiastica auctoritate recognita sit, deseruerit; vel clericales vestes exuerit, quamvis arma non sumpserit et humanum sanguinem minime fuderit; et eo magis qui civili bello sponte sua nomen militiae dederit, aut bellicas actiones quomodocumque dirigere praesumpserit, etsi ecclesiasticum habitum retinere pergat, ab ordinum et graduum exercitio et a quolibet ecclesiastico officio et beneficio suspensus illico et ipso facto maneat."**

In the decree cited here the Supreme Pontiff, Leo XIII, condemned the actions of those clerics who, in violation of the admonitions of the Council of Trent,[82] involve themselves in civil political strifes, which are not uncommon in our day. He forbade clerics to doff the clerical dress or to leave their place of residence for the purpose of engaging in civil wars or other political contentions; neither might they volunteer their services to either side in such wars or even assist in directing the activities of the participants. The penalty incurred *ipso facto* by violating this law was suspension from the exercise of orders and degrees and from all offices and benefices which the delinquent might hold.

This censure has been abrogated by the Legislator, since it is not to be found in the Code of 1918. Can. 141, indeed, strictly forbids clerics to take any part whatsoever in civil wars and other disturbances of the public order. And while no specific punishment is held out for clerics delinquent in this regard, yet they can be duly punished by the Ordinary.[83]

D. New Suspensions.

To complete the present chapter it remains now to consider those censures of suspension which appear for the first time in the Code of 1918. In the course of this chapter we have already had occasion to discuss four of

82 Sess. XIV, in proëm. et cap. 4; Sess. XXII, cap. 1, de ref.; cf. Wernz, II. n. 223 ss.

83 Can. 2222.

this group of censures.[84] The other suspensions which we have quoted from the Code are not true censures, but have been adduced for the purpose of examining the Const. *Apost. Sedis* and other legislation in the light of the new law.[85]

In addition, then to the four already treated, there are found in the Code seven suspensions which are true censures and which are not found in any pre-Code legislation. Of these, one is reserved to the Apostolic See, one to the Ordinary, one to the Proper Superior and four are unreserved. Following the form used throughout the present work, we shall now take up these censûres according to the manner of reservation.

XX. Codex I.C., Can. 2371:

> "Omnes, etiam episcopali dignitate aucti, qui per simoniam ad ordines scienter promoverint vel promoti fuerint aut alia Sacramenta ministraverint vel receperint, sunt suspecti de haeresi; clerici praeterea suspensionem incurrunt Sedi Apostolicae reservatam."

The Church has always detested simony in any form and condemned it in the most vehement terms.[86] As regards simoniacal ordinations, we find legislation as early as the Council of Chalcedon, which declared clerics thus ordained to be deposed and never again promoted. To this penalty was later added suspension and excommunication, especially by Pius V and Sixtus V.[87]

The causes and occasions of simoniacal ordinations having been greatly reduced, Pius IX abrogated, by omitting them from the Const. *Apost. Sedis*, the several censures that were incurred *ipso facto* through that crime.[88]

84 Can. 671, Art. V; Can. 2372, Art. VI; Can. 2409, Art. IX; and Can. 2374, Artt. XI, XIV, and XV.

85 We have already seen that nearly all of the suspensions enumerated in the Const. *Apost. Sedis*, were not medicinal penalties, but vindictive.

86 Cf. Chap. II, Artt. VIII, IX, X.

87 Const. *Cum primum*, Apr. 1, 1566; and Const. *Sanctum et salutare*, Jan. 5, 1589.

88 Wernz, VI, n. 342.

Today the censure of suspension is reinstated in the common law, under Can. 2371. The suspension affects clerics, as distinguished from the laity, the latter being included in the first part of the canon. All clerics are comprehended by the law, and hence even those who have received only the first tonsure. (Can. 108, 1.) Bishops do not incur the suspension, since they are not specified in the canon.[89]

The simony may be "real," in which the pact has been satisfied by both parties, or "mixed," when executed by one party only, but it must be external, i. e., the studied intent to buy or sell the ordination or other sacrament must find expression in some outward action. Mere mental simony, while it is sinful, does not constitute a *delictum.*

It must be noted that there is no simony when an offering is accepted not as a price for, but on the occasion of, certain spiritual administrations, provided there exist a just title, recognized as such by Canon Law or lawful custom.[90] In such a case the temporal thing is given rather as a means of sustenance for the minister whose duty demands him to perform spiritual acts.[91]

Simoniacal administration or reception of the Sacramentals is not a cause for incurring the present censure, since the Code speaks exclusively of the Sacraments. Neither is it incurred unless the administration or reception be performed with full knowledge and deliberation. (Can. 2229, 2.)

89 Can. 2227, 2; the contrary opinion is stated in Noldin, "De Poen. Eccl," n. 118, but it can hardly be sustained. The suspension is here added to the "suspicion of heresy," which clerics are already declared to incur.

90 Can. 730; cf. D'Annibale, "Theol. Moral." III, n. 403 ss.

91 Can. 736: "Pro administratione Sacramentorum minister nihil quavis de causa vel occasione sive directe sive indirecte exigat aut petat, praeter oblationes de quibus in can. 1507, 1." Can. 1507: 1. "Salvo praescripto can. 1056, et can. 1234, praefinire taxas pro variis actibus jurisdictionis voluntariae vel pro executione rescriptorum Sedis Apostolicae vel occasione ministrationis Sacramentorum vel Sacramentalium, in tota ecclesiastica provincia solvendas, est Concilii provincialis aut conventus Episcoporum provinciae; sed nulla vi praefinitio ejusmodi pollet, nisi prius a Sede Apostolica approbata fuerit."

Although the effects of suspension are separable (Can. 2278, 2), the present censure is a general suspension and hence has all the effects that suspension can have. It is reserved in a simple manner to the Holy See; wherefore, if the crime be occult, the delinquent can be absolved by the Ordinary or his delegate. (Can. 2237, 2.)

XXI. Codex I.C., Can. 2341:

> ". . . Si, non obtenta ab Ordinario loci licentia, aliam personam privilegio fori fruentem (ausus fuerit ad judicem laicum trahere) clericus quidem incurrit ipso facto in suspensionem ab officio reservatam Ordinario."[92]

To avoid undue repetition we shall merely refer here to Chap. I, Art. VII, where we discussed the crime of bringing to trial before lay judges, Cardinals, Legates of the Holy See and the Major Officials of the Roman Curia in matters pertaining to their respective offices; and also one's own Ordinary, Titular Bishops, Abbots and Prelates *nullius* and Major Superiors of Pontifical Religions.

Besides these, the privilege of the forum is enjoyed by all clerics after the reception of the first tonsure, all religious of either sex and even novices and lay religious.[93] To cause any of these persons to be summoned as defendants to the lay tribunal, without previously having procured the permission of the Local Ordinary, is the offence that merits the present censure. The Ordinary here intended is he in whose diocese the said tribunal is situated.[94] The suspension is, of course, incurred only by clerics, secular or religious, since this penalty is peculiar to them. Lay persons who offend in this matter are subject to due punishment at the hands of their respective Ordinaries. For both clerics and laity, under

92 The "privilegium fori" of clerics is not recognized by modern civil codes. Cf. "Catholic Encyclopedia," s. v. "Privileges;" Chelodi, l. c., n. 74.

93 Can. 108, 1, 120, 614.

94 Cf. Cerato, n. 124.

the former discipline, the penalty was excommunication *latae sententiae*.[95]

The cleric who falls under the suspension is deprived of all exercise of orders, jurisdiction and administration which he may have, except the administration of his benefice, if he have one,[96] until he obtains absolution, which any Ordinary can impart.

XXII. Codex I.C., Can. 2386:

> "Religiosus fugitivus ipso facto incurrit . . . in suspensionem proprio Superiori majori reservatam, si sit in sacris; . . ."

We saw in Art. VII of Chapter III the penalties incurred by apostate religious. In the present canon we are concerned with fugitives from religion, i. e., "religious who, without the permission of their superiors, desert a religious house with the intention of returning to religion." [97] A perverse intention on the part of the fugitive is here supposed, consisting in the will and desire to evade the obligation of religious obedience.[98] Hence the mere leaving a religious house to which one is attached is not in itself cause for the censure, nor even the leaving of it with the intention of not returning to that house. The religious could hardly be called a fugitive in the present sense (and therefore subject to the censure) who leaves the house to which he is assigned (e. g., because he cannot live agreeably with his superior) and goes to a neighboring house of the same religion, although he does so against the will of his superior and violates his rule. Such a one is not a "deserter." [99]

The suspension, which is reserved to the major Superior[100] of the fugitive religious, is imposed in general

95 Cf. Chap. I, Art. VII.
96 Can. 2279, 1.
97 Can. 644, 3.
98 Cf. Augustine, l. c., III, p. 383.
99 Cf. Blat, "De Personis," p. 630.
100 The Abbot Primates, Abbots who are Superiors of Congregations, Abbots of Monasteries that are independent, although belonging to some Monastic Congregation, the Superior General of any religious society, the Provincial Superiors and their Vicars, and all others who have jurisdiction like to that of Provincials. Can. 488, 8.

terms, and has, therefore, all the effects of suspension.[101] It is incurred as soon as the religious leaves the house with the intention of deserting for a time.

Only religious who have received the sub-diaconate, diaconate or priesthood are liable to the censure. Cerato says[102] the law is restricted to professed religious, but, according to a *Response* given June 23, 1918, by the *Commission for the Authentic Interpretation of the Canons of the Code*, the offense which here merits suspension can be committed also by members of clerical societies in common life, who take no vows.[103]

XXIII. Codex I.C., Can. 2366:

> "Sacerdos qui sine necessaria jurisdictione praesumpserit sacramentales confessiones audire, est ipso facto suspensus a divinis; qui vero a peccatis reservatis absolvere, ipso facto suspensus est ab audiendis confessionibus.

Two distinct censures are here newly enacted for distinct offenses: (a) suspension *a divinis*, i. e., from the exercise of all power of orders, incurred *ipso facto* by a priest[104] who, not having the necessary jurisdiction, presumes to hear sacramental confessions; and (b) suspension from hearing confessions, incurred by a priest who, without the necessary jurisdiction, presumes to absolve from reserved sins.

A. For the valid remission of sins there is required in the minister, besides the power of orders, the power of jurisdiction over the penitent, whether this be ordinary or delegated jurisdiction. (Can. 872.) Priests, secular or religious, even exempt, in order to hear confessions and absolve validly require (except in danger of

101 Can. 2278, 2.

102 N. 123.

103 Cf. A. A. S. IX, p. 344; Chelodi takes this as an "interpretatio extensiva." l. c., n. 101.

104 We have already seen the penalty inflicted upon those not endowed with priestly power who hear sacramental confessions. Can. 2322; cf. Chap. I, Art. XV.

death) delegated jurisdiction, which is granted by the Ordinary of the place where the confessions are to be heard.[105]

Knowingly to hear confessions without ordinary or delegated jurisdiction over the penitent is the offense here punished with suspension *a divinis*. It matters not for what reason the priest lacks jurisdiction, whether because it was never granted him, or because he lost it, or because it does not extend to the time or territory in which he now finds himself, or to the persons upon whom he now attempts to use it, as e. g., in hearing the confessions of religious without the required special delegation. In such cases the Church, when there is common error, supplies the jurisdiction. The absolution is then valid, but this concession of the Church is given in favor of the penitent, not of the priest. His action is unlawful and sinful (unless there be danger of death) and the penalty is incurred.[106]

To incur the censure it is not necessary that absolution be given or even simulated. As Can. 2366 clearly indicates, it suffices to hear confessions which are sacramental, i. e., made by the penitent for the purpose of obtaining absolution.[107] Presumption is required in the offending priest, i. e., he must know that he lacks the necessary jurisdiction and that the hearing of the confession in the circumstance is forbidden under pain of suspension. Ignorance, though it be crass or supine, and light fear excuse from the penalty.[108] Hence the censure is not in-

105 Can. 874, 1. The Code has instituted a considerable change in this matter. Heretofore Religious received their jurisdiction not from the Local Ordinary, but from the Supreme Pontiff, through their Superiors. The approbation of the Ordinary of the place was necessary only for hearing the confessions of seculars. Cf. D'Annibale, "Theol. Moral." III, n. 183; Noldin, l. c., III, n. 359.

106 Can. 209.

107 It is the common teaching of theologians that only those confessions are "sacramental" which are made for the ultimate purpose of obtaining absolution; hence, not those made for seeking counsel, for mere peace of soul, etc. Cf. Suarez, l. c., Disp. XXXII, Sec. 2, n. 7; Lugo, "De Poenit." D. XXIII, Sec. 43, n. 5; S. Alph. l. c., n. 636; D'Annibale l. c., n. 226.

108 Can. 2229, 2.

curred by the priest who acts with doubtful jurisdiction, even when there is no urgent cause for his hearing the confession.[109]

B. The persons who possess ordinary power for granting faculties for hearing confessions[110] can also call to their own tribunal a number of cases, thus restricting the absolving power vested in their inferiors. This "avocatio" or restriction of cases is known as "reservation."[111] The jurisdiction of all inferiors is thereby limited, so that they can no longer exercise any power over the matter which the Superior has reserved to himself. Reservation of sins, however, loses its force when the penitent is in danger of death, in which case any priest, even though he be not approved for hearing confessions, can validly and licitly absolve any penitent from any sin whatsoever, including reserved and notorious cases, and this, even though there be present a priest who is approved for hearing confessions.[112]

Again, all reservation of sins ceases (a) when those who confess are sick and cannot leave their house, or when the penitent is about to be married; (b) as often as the lawful superior refuses the faculty asked for in a particular case, or when, according to the prudent judgment of the confessor, the faculty cannot be asked of the lawful superior without great inconvenience to the penitent or without danger of violating the seal of Confession; (c) outside the territory of the one who has reserved the case, even though the penitent has gone thither for the sole purpose of obtaining absolution. (Can. 900.)

Beyond these instances, if a priest knowingly attempt

109 Cf. D'Annibale, l. c., III, n. 185; S. Alph. l. c., VI, n. 571.

110 This does not include, in the present case, the Vicar Capitular, nor the Vicar General without a special mandate.

111 Can. 893. The reservation should be restricted to three or, at the most, four cases and then only for the more grave and atrocious external crimes, whose nature is to be determined specifically. Moreover, the reservation should end as soon as the specific vice has been extirpated and the discipline restored. Can. 897.

112 Can. 882. However, the requirements of Can. 884, regarding the absolution of an accomplice, must be observed.

to absolve, from a reserved sin, a penitent over whom he has not acquired the jurisdiction necessary for the absolution, he is *ipso facto* suspended from hearing confessions.[113]

Sins may be reserved (a) directly, i. e., on their own account, such as the sin of falsely accusing a priest of the crime of solicitation,[114] and the few sins which Local Ordinaries, Superiors General and Abbots of monasteries *sui juris* may reserve to themselves to extirpate some public vices or to restore discipline; or (b) indirectly, i. e., by reason of a reserved censure which is attached to a sin. Sins reserved in either manner are comprehended by Can. 2366.

The suspension is not incurred unless the priest act with presumption, any diminution of imputability, on the part of either intellect or will, excusing from the penalty.[115] The form of absolution must have been truly pronounced; the mere hearing of the confession or the feigning of absolution would not afford sufficient cause for the suspension.

XXIV. Codex I.C., Can. 2400:

> "Clericus qui in manus laicorum officium, beneficium aut dignitatem ecclesiasticam resignare praesumpserit, ipso facto in suspensionem a divinis incurrit."

Pope Innocent III declared that those who would resign an ecclesiastical benefice into the hands of a lay person were to be deprived of the benefit itself, the transfer to the lay person being invalid.[116] The Code requires that renunciation of an office, benefice or dignity, to be valid, must be presented to the one who has conferred it or to his representative or successor,[117] although tacit renunciation is admitted in law.[118] In any event the competent

113 Cf. Can. 2279, 2, 7.

114 Can. 894. The only sin thus reserved to the Holy See.

115 Can. 2229, 1, 2.

116 C. 8, X, de renunciatione, I, 9.

117 Can. 187.

118 Can. 188.

authority in the matter of ecclesiastical offices, benefices and dignities is the ecclesiastical authority,[119] i. e., the Apostolic See or the Ordinary. "Officium ecclesiasticum nequit sine canonica provisione obtineri." [120]

The resignation which here merits suspension should be a complete, formal and properly so-called resignation. It should be spontaneous on the part of the cleric, not done in fear or ignorance; and should be made personally or at least by a procurator endowed with a special mandate. It should be made under the title of "resignation," in writing, or verbally in the presence of two witnesses;[121] or it may be made in some other manner recognized as valid by the civil law,[122] although, as has been said, the resignation is invalid in Canon Law.

The suspension, which is not reserved, may be incurred by any cleric who holds an office, benefice or dignity in the Church; it forbids every act of the power of orders which the delinquent cleric may have obtained by sacred ordination or by privilege.[123]

XXV. Codex I.C., Can. 2402:

> "Abbas vel Praelatus 'nullius' qui contra praescriptum can. 322, 2, benedictionem non receperit, est ipso facto a jurisdictione suspensus."

The former law on the subject of Abbatial blessing has been considerably clarified by the Code. Formerly, in virtue of the Const. *Commissi Nobis* of Bened. XIII,[124] all Regular Abbots elected for life were obliged, under pain of suspension from office for one year, to receive the blessing as prescribed in the Pontificale Romanum,[125] from the Bishop of the diocese within the space of one year, or at least to ask it of him three times. Abbots and Prelates

119 Can. 1484 ss.
120 Can. 147; Reg. 1, Reg. Jur. in Sexto.
121 Can. 186.
122 Cf. Cerato, l. c., n. 122.
123 Can. 2279, 2, 2.
124 May 6, 1725.
125 De benedictione Abbatis.

nullius might call upon any bishop in union with the Holy See to confer the Abbatial blessing.[126]

Today the Regular Abbot is, indeed, required to receive the blessing, within three months after his lawful election, from the Bishop of the diocese in which his monastery is situated. (Can. 625.) However, only the Abbots and Prelates *nullius* are held to the reception of this blessing under pain of suspension; and even for this three elements must be verified: (a) he must be bound, either by apostolic prescription or by the Constitutions of his own Religion, to receive the blessing according to the form contained in the Pontifical; (b) three months must have elapsed from the reception of the apostolic letters; and (c) the absence of any legitimate impediment that would excuse him. In the presence of these conditions the failure to receive the blessing of any bishop gives rise *ipso facto* to the suspension, so that the Abbot or Prelate *nullius* is forbidden to perform any act of the power of jurisdiction, ordinary or delegated, in the internal as well as the external forum. The censure, while it renders such acts of jurisdiction illicit, does not invalidate them, and can be remitted by a simple confessor.[127]

126 Cf. Wernz, II, n. 387.
127 Cf. Canon 2279, 2, 1.

CHAPTER VII

INTERDICTS

The third and last species of censure with which the Const. *Apost. Sedis* was concerned is Interdict.[1] Two interdicts were expressly mentioned in the Constitution, one of which was reserved in a special manner to the Roman Pontiff. To these were added two interdicts which had been directly enacted by the Council of Trent. These latter, as will be seen presently, have been abrogated by omission from the new Code, while the two interdicts mentioned in the Constitution are renewed, with certain modifications, in the Code, where they are set down in three distinct canons. Finally, we shall see, in the course of this chapter, that one new interdict *latae sententiae* now comes into force, affecting those who give rise to a *local* interdict.

We shall now proceed to consider the interdicts contained in the Constitution, and also the Tridentine interdicts, in the light of the new Code.

I. Const. *Apost. Sedis:*

> "Interdictum Romano Pontifici speciali modo reservatum ipso jure incurrunt Universitates, Collegia et Capitula, quocumque nomine nuncupentur, ab ordinationibus seu mandatis ejusdem Romani Pontificis pro tempore existentis ad Universale futurum Concilium appellantia."

Codex I.C., Can. 2332:

> ". . . Universitates vero, Collegia, Capitula aliaeve personae morales, quocumque nomine nuncupentur, (scl. a legibus, decretis, mandatis Romani

1 The Code departs from the traditional order and places Suspension in the third place, because this is a punishment peculiar to clerics, while Excommunication and Interdict can be incurred by both clerical and lay persons.

> Pontificis pro tempore existentis ad universale Concilium appellantes) interdictum speciali modo Sedi Apostolicae pariter reservatum (ipso facto) incurrunt."

In Art. IV of Chapter I, to which we may here merely refer, lest we repeat unduly, we considered the excommunication incurred by all persons, of whatever rank, station or condition, who appeal to a Universal Council from the laws, decrees or mandates of the Roman Pontiff. That censure, as also the present interdict, was taken from the Bull *In Coena,* Par. 2, having been first decreed by Pope Pius II in the Const. *Execrabilis* Jan. 18, 1459. In the former case, however, we were concerned with individual appellants, who could, therefore, incur the penalty of excommunication. Here we deal with moral persons who commit the same offense, and incur not excommunication, but a *general personal* interdict.

Comparing the old and the new law we find, as was stated in Chapter I, that the word "futurum" has been omitted, so that the appealing to any Ecumenical Council undoubtedly affords sufficient cause for the interdict. Similarly, the Legislator has stated the law more fully so as to include appeals from pontifical "laws" and "decrees" as well as "mandates," because in all these cases the supreme authority of the Pope is equally impugned.

Since it is incumbent upon all persons to respect and observe Pontifical utterances, there has been added to the former law, as regards the present matter, "aliave persona moralis," so that none of those persons are exempt of whom we read in Can. 99: "In Ecclesia praeter personas physicas, sunt etiam personae morales, collegiales et non-collegiales, ut ecclesiae, seminaria, beneficia, etc." "Pious Unions," however, or associations of the faithful organized for the performance of some work of piety or charity, are not included, since they are not moral persons. (Can. 707, 708.)

To incur the interdict it is not necessary that *all* the members appeal. The action of a majority suffices, the blame, however, falling upon the whole moral body.[2] Nevertheless, one who, in this manner, falls under interdict, yet has not participated in placing the cause of it, can, if he is prevented for no other reason, receive the sacraments privately without absolution from the interdict or any other satisfaction.[3]

The question was mooted under the old law whether those incurring this interdict contracted also the censure of excommunication reserved *speciali modo* to the Roman Pontiff.[4] The negative position seems almost certain today because: (a) the excommunication is levied upon those who, as individuals and in their own name, make the appeal, while the interdict affects those who appeal as members of a university, college, or other moral person, and who, therefore, act in the name of the whole moral body; and (b) because, in virtue of Can. 2338, 4, a personal interdict is incurred by those who give cause to the aforesaid interdict, i. e., who actually appeal.[5]

II. Const. *Apost. Sedis:*

> "Scienter celebrantes vel celebrari facientes divina in locis ab Ordinario, vel delegato judice, vel a jure interdictis; aut nominatim excommunicatos ad divina officia, seu ecclesiastica sacramenta, vel ecclesiasticam sepulturam admittentes, interdictum ab ingressu Ecclesiae ipso jure incurrunt, donec ad arbitrium ejus, cujus sententiam contempserunt, competenter satisfecerint."

Codex I.C., Can. 2338, 3:

> "Scienter celebrantes vel celebrari facientes divina in locis interdictis vel admittentes ad celebranda officia divina per censuram vetita clericos excommunicatos, interdictos, suspensos post sententiam declaratoriam vel condemnatoriam, inter-

2 Wernz, VI, n. 223.

3 Can. 2276; cf. Cavigioli, l. c., n. 181.

4 Bucceroni, "Comment. in C. 'Apost. Sedis'," n. 127, and Lehmkuhl, l. c., II, n. 1271, held the affirmative opinion, which was denied by D'Annibale, l. c., n. 158; Pennachi, II, p. 501; and Ball.-Palm., n. 574.

5 Cf. Capello, n. 153.

> dictum ab ingressu ecclesiae ipso jure contrahunt, donec, arbitrio ejus cujus sententiam contempserunt, congruenter satisfecerint."

Can. 2339:

> ". . . sponte vero sepulturam eisdem (scl. qui in can. 1240, 1 enumerantur) donantes, interdictum ab ingressu ecclesiae Ordinario reservatum (contrahunt)."

Three distinct delinquencies are enumerated in the article quoted above: (a) violation of a local interdict; (b) admission of excommunicated persons to the Divine Offices; and (c) admission of these persons to Christian burial. These three offenses are also treated in the Code. The punishment of these offenses by common law is first found in a decree of Pope Boniface VIII,[6] which was modified somewhat, as we shall see, when renewed by Pius IX in 1869. It will be well to consider the delinquencies separately, in order to determine the changes induced by the new law.

A. In the matter of celebrating and having others celebrate the Divine Offices in an interdicted place, the new law simply confirms the old. Clerics alone are liable on the score of celebrating Divine Offices, since these are functions peculiar to clerics. "Celebrare facere" is to induce by command, counsel, request, etc. (and *a fortiori* by threat or force), a person to celebrate who otherwise would not do so.[7] This offense can be committed by laymen, whom we must include under the law since no distinction or restriction of the law, in this regard, can be justified.[8] We must, however, make exception of those days on which, and places in which, the law permits the celebration of certain Divine Offices, but these can be ex-

6 C. 8, de Privilegiis, V, 7, in Sexto.

7 Bucceroni, l. c., n. 128.

8 Chelodi, l. c., n. 72; Cavigioli, l. c., n. 183; Cerato, l. c., n. 114. Contra: Capello, n. 145; cf. also Genicot, l. c., II, n. 625; D'Annibale, l. c., n. 161.

cepted only in so far as the conditions which are set down in the law are observed.[9]

B. A few changes are to be noticed in the law on admitting clerics to the celebration of Divine Offices denied to them by censure. The former law read: "ad divina officia seu ecclesiastica sacramenta," but now, with the comprehensive definition of *divina officia,* as given in the Code (Can. 2256, 1), the specific mention of the Sacraments is not required.

The most important change is that regarding the clerics admitted. Heretofore it was forbidden to admit "nominatim excommunicatos." The law, as we have already said, was originally made in a decree of Boniface VIII,[10] in which it was forbidden also, under the same penalty, to admit clerics who were under interdict. This class was omitted by Pius IX when he published the Const. *Apost. Sedis,* but it is now restored together with that of suspended clerics. However, of each class the law comprehends only those upon whom sentence, declaratory or condemnatory, has been judicially passed.[11] After such sentence excommunicated, suspended and personally interdicted clerics cannot celebrate Divine Offices, nor actively assist at them when this assistance entails participation in the celebration of them, unless the faithful, in danger of death, ask their ministrations. (Cann. 2259-2261, 2274, 2275, 2284.) The status of a suspended cleric is to be determined from the nature of the suspension pronounced upon him.[12] Those under interdict *ab ingressu ecclesiae* are prohibited from celebrating Divine Offices in a church, from which we may infer that his celebrating in an oratory, public, semi-public or private, is permitted.[13]

It is also to be noted that the present penal law comprehends the admission of those clerics only who are by

9 Can. 2271, 2272. Cf. Capello, l. c., n. 155; D'Annibale, l. c., n. 160.

10 C. 8, de Privilegiis, V, 7, in Sexto.

11 Cf. Can. 1868.

12 Cf. 2283, 2284.

13 Cf. Chelodi, l. c., n. 41.

censure denied the right to celebrate Divine Offices, not those laboring under a vindictive punishment. The distinction is made probably because they who admit censured clerics thus hinder them from receding from their contumacy.

The interdict, whether incurred through violation of a local interdict or through the unlawful admission of a cleric under censure, is reserved to the Superior whose sentence (by which the place was interdicted or the cleric excommunicated, interdicted or suspended) has been disregarded; i. e., the interdict lasts until, in the Superior's estimation, fitting satisfaction has been made by the delinquent. This penalty, therefore, in the new Code at least, seems to be rather a "vindictive" penalty than a censure strictly so called.[14]

C. The penal law on the granting of Ecclesiastical Burial has been considerably extended by the new Code. Under the Constitution of Pius IX the law which imposed an interdict *ab ingressu ecclesiae* upon its violators comprehended the burial only of those excommunicated *nominatim*. Today the law extends to all those mentioned in Can. 1240, 1, provided that they have given no sign of repentance. It is, therefore, now forbidden, under pain of the same penalty, freely to grant ecclesiastical burial to

(a) Persons excommunicated or under interdict, upon whom a condemnatory or declaratory sentence has been passed;
(b) Notorious apostates from the faith;[15]
(c) Notorious heretics;
(d) Notorious schismatics;
(e) Notorious members of the Masonic sect and other such associations;

14 While canonists generally have held that the interdict ceases, without absolution, when due satisfaction has been made, yet, if we look upon this penalty as a censure, such a position, in view of Can. 2248, 1,1, is untenable. Chelodi suggests that the Superior grant the faculty of absolving *ad cautelam*. l. c., n. 73.

15 Among these we must number, provided they have been baptized, Rationalists, Free Thinkers, Theoretic Indifferentists, true Modernists in religion, and those who deny the existence or possibility of revelation.

(f) Those who have deliberately committed suicide;
(g) Those who have died in a duel or from a wound received therein;
(h) Those who have ordered that their bodies be cremated; and
(i) Other public and manifest sinners.

The penalty is, as heretofore, interdict *ab ingressu ecclesiae,* which deprives the subject of the right to celebrate or to assist at the Divine Offices in a church, and also the right to ecclesiastical burial itself. Whereas the penalty was formerly reserved to the Superior who had pronounced the sentence of excommunication upon the person unlawfully admitted to burial, it is now reserved to the Ordinary.

The word "sponte" has been inserted in the law to indicate that the interdict is not incurred unless the rector, pastor, etc., act with untrammelled will.[16] Any fear or force or a law of the State, that is brought to bear upon the person who has the power to grant or to deny Christian burial is sufficient to destroy the perfect freedom which the present law requires if the penalty is to be incurred.[17]

The Fathers of the Council of Trent enacted directly two interdicts *latae sententiae,* which, in virtue of the declaration of Pius IX,[18] continued in force after the promulgation of the Const. *Apostolicae Sedis.* These censures, however, find no mention in the new Code, and must, therefore, be considered abrogated. (Can. 6, 5.)

III. The first of these interdicts, which is found in Sess. VI, cap. 1, de ref., could be incurred only by metropolitans and suffragan bishops. The Tridentine law required that residential bishops who were absent from their respective dioceses for more than twelve consecutive months, without sufficient cause, should be reported

16 D'Annibale, (l. c., n. 220) and others held that only grave fear or force would exempt one from the penalty.

17 Cf. Chap. IV, Art. I.

18 Const. *Apost. Sedis.*

to the Supreme Pontiff. The obligation of reporting rested upon the Metropolitan in the case of his suffragans' absence and upon the Suffragan oldest in residence, in the case of an absent Metropolitan. The information was required to be sent to the Supreme Pontiff, under pain of interdict *ab ingressu ecclesiae* within three months after the first year of unlawful absence had elapsed.[19]

While the penalty can no longer be invoked, nevertheless the duty of looking after the observance of the law of residence still devolves upon the above-mentioned persons. Indeed, the denunciation of the offending prelate to the Holy See is now required after an unlawful absence protracted over six continuous months. For we read in Can. 338, 4: "Si ultra sex menses e dioecesi illegitime abfuerint, Episcopum Metropolita, ad normam can. 274, 4,[20] Metropolitam antiquior Suffraganeus residens Sedi Apostolicae denuntiet."

IV. We considered in Chap. VI, Art. IX, the punishment incurred by the Vicar Capitular, or Administrator, who, succeeding to the place of the bishop during the vacancy of a see, grants dimissorial letters to others than those who must receive Orders on account of some benefice which they have obtained or are to obtain, or on account of some certain office in the diocese which must be filled without delay.[21] That law was enacted under Paul III by the Council of Trent, which at the same time declared an interdict to be incurred *ipso facto* by Cathedral Chapters guilty of a like offense.[22] It is with this latter penalty that we are here concerned.

The interdict, as already stated, has been abrogated by the Code. The Cathedral, or the Diocesan Consultors, are obliged to elect, within eight days after they have become aware of the see's vacancy, a Vicar Capitular, or

19 Cf. Pennachi, II, p. 518 ss.

20 "In dioedesibus vero suffraganeis Metropolita potest.... vigilare ut fides ac disciplina ecclesiastica accurate serventur, ac de abusibus Romanum Pontificem certiorem facere."

21 Cf. Can. 958, 2

22 Sess. VII, cap. 10, de ref; sess. XXIII, cap. 10, de ref.

Administrator, to rule the diocese in place of the bishop.[23] The Vicar Capitular, or Administrator, cannot, within the first year of the vacancy, grant dimissorial letters, except for the reasons recited above. Upon him a penalty is inflicted if he grant such letters in any other case. The penalty, which was formerly suspension from office and benefice, is now suspension *a divinis*, or the privation of the right to exercise any power of Orders which he may have received by ordination or by privilege. (Can. 2409.)

V. One new interdict *latae sententiae* has been instituted by the new Code.

Can. 2338, 4:

> "Qui causam dederunt interdicto locali aut interdicto in communitatem seu collegium, sunt ipso facto personaliter interdicti."

This penalty is newly established in accordance with the general principle set down in the Code (Can. 2218) that the punishment of an offense should be proportionate to the offense committed. Now, those who commit the act whereby an interdict falls upon a place or upon a community or a college are personally guilty. Yet, as residents of the place or as members of the community or college they suffer no more than do the innocent residents or members. We can readily see, then, the purpose of the Legislator in establishing this personal interdict as a special punishment to be incurred by one who causes a local or a general personal interdict, whether this be *latae sententiae* or *ferendae sententiae*.[24]

23 Can. 432 ss. Conc. Trid. Sess. XXIV, cap. 16, de ref.
24 Cf. Cerato, n. 115; Capello, n. 158.

APPENDIX I

The following summary will serve to illustrate the general effect of the new Code with respect to censures *latae sententiae* contained in the common law of the Church.

CENSURES

Reserved To	In force up to Pentecost 1918 (1)	Abrogated by Code	Instituted by Code	Now in force
Excommunications:				
Apost. See concerning election of Rom. Pont.	10			10
Apost. See *specialissimo modo*	1		3	4
Apost. See *speciali modo*	12	2	2	12
Apost. See *simpliciter*	18	6	1	13
Ordinary	4	1	6	9
Unreserved	17	12		5
Suspensions:				
Apost. See	8	7	3	4
Ordinary	4	4	1	1
Maj. Rel. Superior			1	1
Unreserved	7	4	3	6
Interdicts:				
Apost. See *speciali modo*	1			1
Ordinary			1	1
Superior imposing interdict	1			1
Unreserved	2	2	1	1

(1) This list includes the censures contained, explicitly or implicitly, in the Const. *Apost. Sedis* and those subsequently instituted.

APPENDIX II

The following is a complete enumeration of the censures *latae sententiae* which are now to be found in the general law of the Church. The censures are here grouped as they were in the Constitution *Apostolicae Sedis,* in order to facilitate the comparison of the former and the present law.

EXCOMMUNICATIONS

Excommunication reserved to the Apostolic See *specialissimo modo.* Incurred by:

1. Those who throw away the Consecrated Hosts, or carry them away or keep them for an evil purpose. Can. 2320.
2. Those who lay violent hands on the person of the Roman Pontiff. Can. 2344.
3. Confessors absolving or pretending to absolve an accomplice *in peccato turpi.* Can. 2367.
4. Confessors who directly violate the seal of confession. Can. 2369.

(For excommunications incurred in connection with the election of the Roman Pontiff, see the Const. *Vacante Sede Apostolica,* which is appended to the Canons in the Code. Nos. 37, 50, 51, 52, 69, 79, 80, 81, 82 and 88.)

Excommunication reserved to the Apostolic See *speciali modo.* Incurred by:

1. Apostates *a fide,* Heretics and Schismatics. Can. 2314.
2. Persons suspected of heresy who, after six months, have shown no signs of amendment. Can. 2315.
3. Editors of books of apostates, heretics and schismatics, and those who defend, read or retain such books or others which the Holy See has prohibited. Can. 2318, 1.
4. Persons who, not being ordained priests, pretend to celebrate Mass or hear sacramental confessions. Can. 2322, 1.

5. Those who appeal to a General Council from the laws, decrees or mandates of the Roman Pontiff. Can. 2332.
6. Those who, by recourse to the civil power, obstruct the letters or acts of the Apostolic See or its Legates. Can. 2333.
7. Those who publish laws, decrees or mandates against liberty or rights of the Church; or who, by recourse to the lay power, impede the exercise of ecclesiastical jurisdiction. Can. 2334.
8. Those who bring suit, before a lay judge, against a Cardinal, Apostolic Legate, major official of the Roman Curia or their own Ordinary. Can. 2341.
9. Those who lay violent hands on a Cardinal, Legate, Patriarch, Archbishop or Bishop. Can. 2343, 2, 3.
10. Usurpers or holders of property or rights belonging to the Roman Church. Can. 2345.
11. Those who forge or falsify letters, decrees or rescripts of the Apostolic See, or who knowingly use such false documents. Can. 2360, 1.
12. Those who falsely charge a confessor *de sollicitando.* Can. 2363.

Excommunication reserved to the Apostolic See *simpliciter*. Incurred by:

1. Those who traffic in indulgences. Can. 2327.
2. Members of the Masonic sect or similar associations. Can. 2335.
3. Confessors who, without the necessary faculties, presume to absolve from excommunication reserved to the Apostolic See in a special or very special manner. Can. 2338, 1.
4. Those who aid an *excommunicatus vitandus* in *crimine criminoso;* clerics who communicate with such person *in divinis.* Can. 2338, 2.
5. Those who bring suit, before a lay judge, against a Bishop (not *proprius*), Abbot or Prelate *nullius,* or certain Religious Superiors. Can. 2341.

6. Those who, without permission, enter the cloister of nuns; those who admit such persons. Can. 2342, 1.
7. Women who enter the cloister of Regulars, and Superiors and others who admit them. Can. 2342, 2.
8. Nuns who leave cloister (Papal) without due permission. Can. 2342, 3.
9. Usurpers or unjust holders of ecclesiastical property. Can. 2346.
10. Duellers, and those who aid, view, or permit duels. Can. 2351, 1.
11. Clerics in Sacred Orders and Religious with solemn vows who attempt marriage, and those who contract with them. Can. 2388, 1.
12. Those who commit simony in connection with any ecclesiastical office, benefice or dignity. Can. 2392.
13. Vicars Capitular (Administrators) and others who remove, destroy, conceal or substantially change any document belonging to the Episcopal Curia. Can. 2405.

Excommunication reserved to the Ordinary. Incurred by:

1. Catholics who give or renew the matrimonial consent before a non-Catholic minister acting as such. Can. 2319, 1, 1.
2. Catholics who contract marriage with the understanding, implicit or explicit, that any or all of the children will be educated outside the Catholic Church. Can. 2319, 1, 2.
3. Catholics who knowingly present their children to a non-Catholic minister for Baptism. Can. 2319, 1, 3.
4. Catholic parents and *locum tenentes* who knowingly hand over children in their charge to be educated in a non-Catholic religion. Can. 2319, 1, 4.
5. Those who manufacture false relics or who knowingly sell, distribute or expose them for public veneration. Can. 2326.

6. Those who lay violent hands upon clerics or religious. Can. 2343, 4.
7. Those who procure abortion. Can. 2350, 1.
8. Apostates *a religione*. Can. 2385.
9. Religious with simple perpetual vows who contract marriage, and those who contract with them. Can. 2388, 2.

Excommunication unreserved. Incurred by:

1. Authors and editors who, without due permission, have the Sacred Scriptures printed, or even annotations or commentaries thereon. Can. 2318, 2.
2. Those who command or force ecclesiastical burial to be given to persons prohibited by law. Can. 2339.
3. Those who alienate ecclesiastical property without the necessary permission of the Apostolic See. Can. 2347, 3.
4. Those who force others into religion or the clerical state. Can. 2352.
5. Penitents who refuse to denounce a confessor guilty of solicitation. Can. 2368, 2.

SUSPENSIONS

Suspension reserved to the Apostolic See. Incurred by:

1. Dismissed religious. Can. 671, 1.
2. Bishop and those assisting, who consecrate a bishop without the Apostolic mandate; and also the bishop consecrated. Can. 2370.
3. Clerics who, through simony, are promoted to Orders or receive or administer any other Sacrament. Can. 2371.
4. Those who knowingly receive Orders from a prelate upon whom sentence of censure has been passed, or whose apostasy, heresy or schism is notorious. Can. 2372.

Suspension reserved to the Ordinary. Incurred by:

1. Clerics who bring suit, before a lay judge, against a cleric or a religious. Can. 2341.

Suspension reserved to the Major Religious Superior. Incurred by:

1. Fugitive religious. Can. 2386.

Suspension unreserved. Incurred by:

1. Priests who knowingly hear sacramental confessions without the necessary jurisdiction. Can. 2366.
2. Priests who knowingly absolve from reserved sins without the necessary jurisdiction. Can. 2366.
3. Those who advance to Orders without due dimissorial letters or before the canonical age or *per saltum.* Can. 2374.
4. Clerics who knowingly resign an ecclesiastical office, benefice or dignity into the hands of laymen. Can. 2400.
5. Abbots or Prelates *nullius* who do not receive the episcopal blessing within the stated time. Can. 2402.
6. Vicars Capitular (Administrators) who grant dimissorial letters contrary to law. Can. 2409.

INTERDICTS

Interdict reserved to the Apostolic See *speciali modo.* Incurred by:

1. Universities, Colleges, Chapters and other moral persons who appeal to a General Council from the laws, decrees or mandates of the Roman Pontiff. Can. 2332.

Interdict reserved to the Ordinary. Incurred by:

1. Those who freely grant ecclesiastical burial to persons prohibited by law. Can. 2339.

Interdict reserved to the superior whose sentence has been disregarded. Incurred by:

1. Those who violate a local interdict or permit certain violations of personal interdict. Can. 2338, 3.

Interdict unreserved. Incurred by:

1. Those who cause a local or a general personal interdict. Can. 2338, 4.

DEUS LUX MEA

CANONES

QUOS

AD DOCTORATUS GRADUM

IN

JURE CANONICO

APUD UNIVERSITATEM CATHOLICAM AMERICAE

CONSEQUENDUM

PUBLICE PROPUGNABIT

GEORGIUS LEO LEECH

SACERDOS ARCHIDIOECESIS PHILADELPHIENSIS

JURIS CANONICI LICENTIATUS

Hora IX Die XXIX Maii A. D. MCMXXII

Universitas Catholica Americae
Washingtonii, D. C.
Sacra Facultas Theologica
1921-1922
No. 15

CANONES

I. Canones 1-7. De Codicis ambitu.
II. " 8-11. De legibus ecclesiasticis in genere.
III. " 12-14. De legum ecclesiasticarum subjectis.
IV. " 15-16. De legum effectibus.
V. " 17-24. De legis interpretatione.
VI. " 25-30. De consuetudine.
VII. " 31-35. De temporis supputatione.
VIII. " 36-62. De rescriptis.
IX. " 63-79. De privilegiis.
X. " 82-86. De dispensationibus.
XI. " 87-89. De personis in genere.
XII. " 90-95. De domicilio et quasi-domicilio.
XIII. " 108-110. De clericis in genere.
XIV. " 111-117. De clericorum adscriptione.
XV. " 118-123. De juribus et privilegiis clericorum.
XVI. Canon 145. De officii ecclesiastici notione.
XVII. Canones 196-210. De potestate ordinaria et delegata.
XVIII. " 215-217. De divisione dioecesarum.
XIX. " 356-362. De synodo dioecesana.
XX. " 385-390. De examinatoribus synodalibus et parochis consultoribus.
XXI. " 824-844. De Missarum eleemosynis seu stipendiis.
XXII. " 845-851. De ministro sacrae communionis.
XXIII. " 893-900. De reservatione peccatorum.
XXIV. " 938-939. De ministro extremae unctionis.

XXV. Canones 1012-1015. De natura matrimonii ejusque divisione.
XXVI. " 1035-1042. De impedimentis in genere.
XXVII. " 1060-1064. De impedimento mixtae religionis.
XXVIII. " 1133-1137. De convalidatione simplici.
XXIX. " 1138-1141. De sanatione in radice.
XXX. " 1239-1242. De sepultura ecclesiastica.
XXXI. " 1552-1554. De judicii ecclesiastici notione, objecto et divisione.
XXXII. " 1594-1596. De tribunali secundae instantiae.
XXXIII. " 1636-1639. De loco et tempore judicii.
XXXIV. " 1679-1683. De actione ob nullitatem actorum.
XXXV. " 1690-1692. De mutuis petitionibus.
XXXVI. " 1825-1828. De praesumptionibus.
XXXVII. " 1960-1965. De foro competenti in causis matrimonialibus.
XXXVIII. " 1986-1989. De appellatione in causis matrimonialibus.
XXXIX. " 1990-1992. De processu administrativo in causis matrimonialibus.
XL. " 2186-2194. De suspensione ex informata conscientia.
XLI. " 2195-2198. De notione delicti ejusque divisione.
XLII. " 2209 et 2211 et 2231. De complicibus in delicto.
XLIII. " 2215-2219. De poenarum notione, speciebus, interpretatione atque applicatione.
XLIV. " 2236-2240. De poenarum remissione.
XLV. " 2241-2244. De censuris in genere.

XLVI. Canones 2245-2254. De censurarum reservatione et absolutione.
XLVII. " 2257-2267. De excommunicatione.
XLVIII. " 2268-2277. De interdicto.
XLIX. " 2278-2285. De suspensione.
L. " 2306-2311. De remediis poenalibus.
LI. " 2314-2316. De haeresi.
LII. Canon 2319. De haeresi faventibus.
LIII. " 2339. De sepultura ecclesiastica.
LIV. " 2341. De privilegii fori violatione.
LV. " 2347. De alienatione bonorum ecclesiasticorum.
LVI. " 2350. De crimine abortus.
LVII. " 2367. De absolutione complicis.
LVIII. " 2368. De crimine solicitationis.
LIX. " 2369. De violatione sigilli sacramentalis.
LX. 2404-2414. De abusu potestatis vel officii ecclesiastici.

Vidit Sacra Facultas:
Carolus F. Aiken, S.T.D., *p. t. Decanus.*
H. Schumacher, S.T.D., *p. t. a Secretis.*

Vidit Rector Universitatis:
+Thomas J. Shahan, S.T.D.

www.ingramcontent.com/pod-product-compliance
Lightning Source LLC
LaVergne TN
LVHW050230080826
844660LV00012B/507

* 9 7 8 0 8 1 3 2 2 2 0 6 6 *